HOW not *IF*

to Navigate Difficult Conversations

by Bridget DiCello

Cover artwork by Design the Planet, New Orleans, LA.
Mountain image by Jodi Brown, New Orleans, LA.

ISBN-10: 0985299509
EAN-13: 9780985299507
LCCN: 2012934924
Building Bridges, LLC

*This book is dedicated to my children,
Megan, Aedan and Cayleigh. May it offer insights
that enable you to continually reach for your potential,
master difficult conversations and build powerful
relationships so that challenging situations
never hold you back.*

Table of Contents

HOW not IF

Introduction

How, not *If*

This book is a collection of articles focused on addressing the communication challenges faced every day in the world of leadership and management. The challenges are difficult to the point that as a leader, you may choose whether or not to even address them. However, the defining difference of the effective leader's approach is that they will determine 'How' to fix the situation, not 'If' it should be addressed. The effective leader knows they need to resolve each roadblock to ensure their success. After reading the article about 'If' and 'How' leaders, consider which type of leader you are and which you prefer to be.

How to Use This Book

Designed as a resource book, you can use the Table of Contents or Index to pinpoint articles relevant to your current situation, read each in under a minute and obtain insight valuable to your effectiveness. Each of the eleven sections includes articles in a specific area where you face difficult conversations. Listed below each article title in the table of contents are multiple concepts addressed in that article. You can use this information to assist you in identifying which articles will help you in a given situation.

It is difficult to manage people, and rarely is it a fully inborn set of skills. Leaders are most often created through much hard work on their part. And it is possible and much easier to lead your team if you can master the art of communication in a variety of situations.

Take a moment to rate yourself on your current level of effectiveness in each of the areas below. Then identify five leadership skills you wish to improve. After using the insights, checklists and reference articles included in this book, rate yourself again, noting your level of improvement and your specific progress.

Currently	Skill	After Focus & Hard Work	Progress
1 2 3 4 5	Accountability	1 2 3 4 5	——— ———
1 2 3 4 5	Conflict Resolution	1 2 3 4 5	——— ———
1 2 3 4 5	Decision Making	1 2 3 4 5	——— ———
1 2 3 4 5	Problem Solving	1 2 3 4 5	——— ———

1 2 3 4 5 Asking   1 2 3 4 5   ————————
          Questions   ————————

1 2 3 4 5 Listening   1 2 3 4 5   ————————
                                        ————————

1 2 3 4 5 Personality   1 2 3 4 5   ————————
          Style   ————————

1 2 3 4 5 Coaching   1 2 3 4 5   ————————
                                        ————————

1 2 3 4 5 Performance   1 2 3 4 5   ————————
          Evaluations   ————————

1 2 3 4 5 Recognition   1 2 3 4 5   ————————
                                        ————————

1 2 3 4 5 Innovation   1 2 3 4 5   ————————
                                        ————————

1 2 3 4 5 Professional 1 2 3 4 5   ————————
          Development   ————————

1 2 3 4 5 Facilitating 1 2 3 4 5   ————————
          Change   ————————

1 2 3 4 5 Setting Goals 1 2 3 4 5   ————————
                                        ————————

1 2 3 4 5 Sharing Goals 1 2 3 4 5   ————————
                                        ————————

1 2 3 4 5 Achieving   1 2 3 4 5   ————————
          Goals   ————————

1 2 3 4 5 Leadership   1 2 3 4 5   ————————
          Ability   ————————

1 2 3 4 5 Management   1 2 3 4 5   ————————
          Ability   ————————

1 2 3 4 5 Confrontation 1 2 3 4 5   ————

————

1 2 3 4 5 Breaking 1 2 3 4 5   ————
Down Walls

————

1 2 3 4 5 Being a 'How' 1 2 3 4 5   ————
Leader

————

1 2 3 4 5 Job 1 2 3 4 5   ————
Descriptions

————

1 2 3 4 5 Productivity 1 2 3 4 5   ————

————

1 2 3 4 5 Employee 1 2 3 4 5   ————
Engagement

————

1 2 3 4 5 Diffusing 1 2 3 4 5   ————
Tension

————

1 2 3 4 5 Focus on 1 2 3 4 5   ————
Results

————

1 2 3 4 5 Tracking 1 2 3 4 5   ————
Metrics

————

1 2 3 4 5 Meeting 1 2 3 4 5   ————
Agendas

————

1 2 3 4 5 Building 1 2 3 4 5   ————
Relationships

————

1 2 3 4 5 Leading 1 2 3 4 5   ————
Meetings

————

1 2 3 4 5 Building Trust 1 2 3 4 5   ————

————

1 2 3 4 5 Critical Feedback	1 2 3 4 5	_____ _____
1 2 3 4 5 Identifying Next Steps	1 2 3 4 5	_____ _____
1 2 3 4 5 Setting Expectations	1 2 3 4 5	_____ _____
1 2 3 4 5 Interviewing	1 2 3 4 5	_____ _____
1 2 3 4 5 Time Management	1 2 3 4 5	_____ _____

Leadership takes a lifetime to perfect. Great leaders never stop learning and acknowledge each step they take to climb that mountain. Climbing a mountain is an effective analogy for moving from being a good leader to being a great leader. No matter how good of a climber you are, you still take it one step at a time. Your steps may be quicker than someone else, but if you take your eyes off where you are going to put your foot next, you could slip and fall. The mountain image at the beginning of each article reminds you to target what piece of progress you hope to make today and identify what piece of progress you made yesterday. You will successfully climb the mountain of leadership development with that thought process.

Take Action

At the end of each article is an opportunity for you to list three action items. These are specific things that you will do right away to implement the ideas and concepts from that particular article. As you read an article that applies to your current challenges, take a moment to identify the first steps you can take to implement change. Refer to them at a later date, acknowledge your progress, and identify the next steps to climbing your mountain.

HOW not IF

Becoming a More Effective Leader
Section Overview

Navigating Difficult Conversations

Difficult conversations are difficult. Why? Because conversations take place between people who differ in their frames of reference, opinions, expectations, beliefs, experiences, attitudes, approaches and styles. Even if a relationship between two people is very amiable, a difficult conversation may occur if a situation arises where one person is expected to change their mindset, performance or boundaries. Change is very difficult for virtually everyone. Successful leaders still have a comfort zone within which they prefer to remain, even if they have effectively expanded that zone beyond that of the average leader.

When you find yourself in a difficult conversation, consider why that occurs:

- When one person is challenged by another person, they tend to get defensive, jealous, nervous, impatient and even excited. Some people like to talk in order to think, and some would rather think before they talk. These different styles can make a seemingly easy conversation very difficult.

- People's emotions are present in every conversation. In a difficult conversation, both people are navigating a mine field, where they are unsure when and if the other person may explode with excitement, blow up in anger or take off on a tangent.

- People, when in a difficult situation, may choose to be silent and refuse to actively participate, or yell in anger or frustration. Whenever communication is interrupted in this way, the conversation automatically becomes difficult.

- Most people, in conversation, will withhold some information from the other person for a variety of reasons. They may do this because it slipped their mind or because they think sharing it will make them vulnerable. Missing information means the conversation is not firing on all cylinders.

In a conversation, each person may have different expectations, desires and end results on which they depend. Each person's expectations of the conversation may not be clear to them or to others. Communicating something from your mind and ensuring it reaches the other person's mind can be a long and treacherous journey. In general, when we communicate:

1. we may not say what we mean.

2. we don't hear what the other person means to say.

3. words, statements, sentences and accusations all have connotations – what words mean to us and to others.

When you consider these realities, it's surprising we ever have calm and productive conversations!

Real Conversations

Many people never have what I call *real conversations* where issues are discussed, frustrations are voiced and resolved, conclusions are made and next steps are agreed upon. Real conversations require a level of ability to address conflict, continue to communicate in a tense situation and persevere to achieve the desired end result.

Difficult conversations occur in each of the key things you must do to manage employees well. The desire to communicate more effectively requires a change in mindset and a change in approach. Muster the determination to move past deciding 'If' you will engage in these difficult conversations and focus on 'How' to make that happen.

Finally, professionals often assume the *leader* is a great communicator and the *manager* is the mean one who carries a big stick. Not so. The final article in the introductory section points out the benefits of both hats worn by those in supervisory roles.

Difficult conversations happen all the time. Use this book as a resource and improve your skills in a variety of situations where conversations may become difficult. Your business results, personal stress level, employee engagement and team morale will significantly improve.

With the determination to become a more effective leader, let's explore 'How,' not 'If' to get it done, one step at a time.

Three Main Types of Difficult Conversations

The Accountability Conversation

The Accountability Conversation is one of the most difficult and that is why it fails to routinely occur in many companies. It is a conversation in which the employee must answer for how well their performance matches expectations that have been set. This conversation often comes before the disciplinary situation where you'd like to fire the person. It both acknowledges their contributions and addresses their shortcomings in productivity or effectiveness. It occurs during the normal course of doing business and should be held on an ongoing basis. It will not be a surprise to the employee if you have set the expectation that it is part of their aggressive individual plan to achieve excellence.

With that said, start by asking yourself these questions:

- What is the specific unacceptable behavior that is causing the problem with performance? Define the *specific* behavior and avoid accusatory adjectives like "grumpy, bad attitude, lacks initiative, or lazy."

- Does the employee know your expectations? When have you told them? Did they understand you clearly?

- Has their current performance been acceptable in the past?

Accountability works best when both the manager and the employee expect it to occur, there is a set routine, and both people are actively involved. These are the most important steps:

1. Be sure to clearly explain what is expected. More detail may be required for some front line employees. Higher level employees may have more freedom in how to do the job and their expectations are more focused on results than tasks.

2. 'Test' understanding. Not by asking them to repeat what you said, but by asking a question that requires they speak about what they will do first, or what they expect to be most difficult.

3. Set a time and date for follow-up. Make sure they realize what they will have been expected to accomplish by that time. This may be a specific result, progress they will have been expected to make or a task that should be finished.

4. Adhere to the time and date you establish. At that set time, ask them to report on their progress, without prodding them with a lot of questions.

5. Continue the accountability by setting the next milestones and corresponding accountability dates. Have these types of conversations routinely, taking just a moment to do so or setting a sit-down meeting.

The Confrontation Conversation

The Confrontation Conversation is dreaded by many because it may appear to start a 'fight.' You may be tempted to 'leave well enough alone.' However, if you are forward looking and have a brighter future in your mind for what is possible, it's essential.

Knowing that, start by asking yourself these questions:

- Do I need to address this issue? Choose your battles carefully. A problem ignored can blow up later. However, nitpicking every detail will wear out any relationship.

- Am I the right person to address the issue? Is there someone else to whom the person reports on this issue? Is there someone who has a better working relationship and is in an appropriate position to address it?

- Is now the right time to address it? Are they as open and receptive as they ever will be? Will waiting let the situation get worse or the impact of the conversation be less?

When you address a situation that you expect to be confrontational, take a moment of Opportunity

Space™, the moment between when someone does or says something and you respond, and ask yourself The Three Questions:

1. What do I really want to accomplish in the long term? Keep your long term objectives in the forefront of your mind and don't be side tracked with the emotion of the moment.

2. Where are they coming from? Why is it that they are doing the things they are doing? What does the situation look like from their perspective?

3. How am I making them feel? However they are feeling is okay, so avoid telling them not to feel the way they feel. It's what they do as a result that can become unacceptable.

If the confrontation goes badly, you might need to take a break and come back and address it when emotions have calmed down. If the person is upset and responds angrily, that might be a defense mechanism to avoid having the conversation. In that case, any break taken should be short and have the specific purpose of giving everyone time to calm down and come back to finish the conversation productively.

The 'Breaking Down Walls' Conversation

The 'Breaking Down Walls' Conversation is one that has the potential to take working relationships to the next level. You may be in a situation that is not great, but is not that bad either, it's just tense. This tension occurs routinely when people interact with one another. It becomes a problem when it continues unaddressed, nothing eases the tension, or when the tension escalates.

With that said, start by asking yourself these questions:

- Is it important I break down this wall? Or is it temporary and will go away on its own?

- What created the wall in the first place? Was it something I did? Was it something they did? Was it external to work? Was it job pressure of some sort?

- What is the opinion of someone I trust about the situation? Do they think this is a real wall?

- Where is the person on the other side of the wall coming from?

Walls can be a problem if they keep the work from being done and prevent positive results from being accomplished. They can also be a problem if they cause an uncomfortable situation for those involved.

It is important to 'clear the air.' If two employees are in conflict, a manager can talk to each one separately. Or talk to them together and mediate. Talking to the two separately can put the manager in the position where each employee tries to win them over. Then again, the individuals may get very upset if confronted together.

The best way to deal with the situation:

1. First talk with each person involved and help them to understand their situation, assuring

them you will not be the final judge, just the mentor and coach. Help them to answer the questions above, keeping the conversation focused on them, how they see it, what they have done and what they can and will do differently.

2. Then, bring both the people together and set some clear ground rules to ensure they understand that this is not an opportunity to personally attack the other person, but a time to look at how the situation arose and what each person will do to diffuse it. Keep the long term objective, company goals, customer service or similar end goal, as the focus of why they need to work together better.

Reading inspires thought.
Thought leads to ideas.
Ideas generate action.
Action happens one step at a time.
The first step is the most difficult to determine and to take.

What are the first steps you will take as a result of reading this article?

1. _____
2. _____
3. _____

Are you an "IF" or a "HOW" Leader?

Leaders strive to bring out the best in their people, and focus on increasing motivation and initiative of team members. Are you and your team of managers leading your employees in a way that enables them to discover their potential?

When presented with either a great idea or innovative strategy, or faced with a challenge, are you an 'If' or a 'How' Leader?

The 'If' Leader

The 'If' Leader seeks the answer to the question, "Can we do it?" Based on known strengths and weaknesses, your team will look at what they consider to be the viability of the idea or strategy, or enormity of the challenge. They will make a list of the pros and cons of the idea or the obstacles and opportunities surrounding the challenge. Often the 'If' Leader will create a risk-averse team focused on the obstacles and drawbacks. This environment is not conducive to the risk-taker who has an approach that just might work but requires everyone to be engaged and excited. The result is a

"Yes" or "No" answer to the question, "Can we do it?"
The underlying assumption is that we are determining
if we can or we can't.

The 'How' Leader

*The 'How' Leader dives into how it could be done, despite obstacles,
and encourages people to think about "How could we do it?"*

This team comes up with possibilities of how it can be
accomplished. The fact that each of the team members
are actively engaged in thinking about options means
that more methods are presented and the situation is
better understood. The result is multiple possibilities,
and the underlying assumption is that we can if we
want to. The side benefit is that everyone is involved
in thinking about 'How' it could be done and their
thinking about the possibilities engage them more in
their day-to-day work. Then, the question becomes,
"Do we *want* to do it?" based on the risks, costs,
projected benefits and fit with company focus. *The
decision-making power is in the hands of the team.*

It's important to weigh pros and cons. There is also
great potential in engaging employees to think about
options instead of simply deciding to open or close a
door. At the same time, it is not necessary to spend a
great deal of everyone's time on a crazy idea or ignore
real obstacles or roadblocks.

As the leader, something as simple as which one
of these two questions you ask regularly can create
two very different teams. If you and your team of

managers don't teach your employees how to think by asking them to do so on a regular basis, you may never access the best within them. The same is true for participants on a team. You can positively affect team dynamics by bringing a 'How' focus to the team.

Which question do you ask? Which question do the members of your team ask most often?

1 – The 'If' Leader asks, "Can we do it?"

2 – The 'How' Leader asks, "How could we do it?" and, "Do we want to do it, given the options?"

How, not If - Good Questions to ask.

There are times when your team decides it is an 'If' situation and you feel it is a 'How' situation. Here are questions and dialog suggestions when you have decided you *will* be successful and just need to determine how.

Be sure to ask all questions with genuine curiosity.

- I understand you have some concerns about Project A. Can you tell me more about them?

- Project A is considered a high priority to a lot of people. It sounds like you feel that other projects are higher priority. Can you share with me your thoughts on that?

- So, if I understand you correctly, you see Project A as near impossible to complete/complete on time? Tell me more about that.

- Can you tell me about the work you have put into Project A to this point?

- What successes have you experienced so far?

- What do you see as good reasons to do Project A?

- I really appreciate you sharing your concerns with me. Project A is considered a top priority for our department. It is important because it enables us to serve our customers better, faster and cheaper. If we don't get it done and done on time, we could lose significant market share.

  - As a valuable member of the team, I really need you to actively participate in getting it done. I'd like to have a discussion with you about all the possible options for getting it done and done on time. I know you have the ability to generate some unique ideas. What do you see as the first step to getting started?

- I'd like to stop discussing whether or not we can do it, and start discussing how we will do it. You start.

- A brilliant mathematician once claimed that there are at least six solutions to every problem. I'd like to hear what you think are the six possibilities. *Employee starts and gets stuck.*

  - Good start. Let's just say the deadline is not movable, what are a few crazy ideas for how we could possibly get it done?

- Let's just say that we must deliver exactly what we initially promised. What could we do then?

Reading inspires thought.
Thought leads to ideas.
Ideas generate action.
Action happens one step at a time.
The first step is the most difficult
to determine and to take.

What are the first steps you will take as a result of reading this article?

1. _____
2. _____
3. _____

Managing Those Who Drive You Crazy

Each person is a unique individual who approaches and responds to life – their job, their tasks, their family, stress and pressure – differently. However, you may have noticed that certain people seem to gel with you and others drive you insane. Maybe no one drives you insane, and that's part of your uniqueness.

Imagine you are focused on aggressively increasing sales and have engaged your entire team in this initiative. Below I describe four behavior styles/personalities that you may see in your organization.

Larry wants to know specifically where you want to increase sales, by how much and by when. He would like to be given his assignment without lengthy explanation or discussion and not be required to work with anyone else on the project. And when he finishes this particular project, it will be on time and well done. He expects his performance to be compared to others' performance, and his successes rewarded. He wants to be able to delegate the follow-up details and move on to the next assignment. Unfortunately, Larry will annoy people in the process, leave some in the dust and take all the credit.

Monica has some great ideas of how the company can grow. She wants to know when everyone can sit down together and talk about them – and she's bringing the refreshments. She's great at getting everyone excited about their role in the initiative. Then, she'll plan the follow-up meeting to celebrate progress and motivate everyone to maintain enthusiasm. Unfortunately, Monica's discussions may never produce great results and although everyone's happy, we'll all cry together if the company doesn't grow.

Conner is comfortable with what we are doing right now and follows the system faithfully. He can see how the current system could use a little tweaking to produce more growth. During the meeting to discuss new initiatives, Conner routinely volunteers to help and support others in the growth initiatives. When Conner offers to help, everyone knows it will get done. Unfortunately, Conner's not that driven to step out of his comfort zone to try something new, especially if he must confront others about doing their part.

Matthew feels it is very important to gather all the data about how we are currently performing and what is currently working before we start talking about how to change. He researches, gathers and sends this detailed information to everyone before the meeting and asks everyone to review it and be prepared to discuss it in detail. Of the ideas generated at the meeting, Matthew takes notes and assigns someone to research and explore each of the possibilities. Unfortunately, if Matthew's in charge, his level of analyzing may mean we never implement any changes or the scenery may change by the time he feels we understand it enough to make a move.

- Which of these people drive you crazy?

- Who is on your team?

- With which of these people do you really enjoy working?

- Do you wish you had a whole team of one type?

- Do you wish you could get rid of one of these people entirely?

Sometimes we think we have the wrong person in our organization, when really we just don't know how to manage them.

Most teams have all of the above characters in the mix. Managing them well first means you need to understand you, and then you need to understand them – all while focusing on what you want to achieve. If this is a struggle for you, find some help, read the plethora of resources on behavior styles, and work with a coach on looking at your team and maximizing their performance. Do something to make sure it doesn't drive you crazy, your team functions well and you succeed!

Reading inspires thought.
Thought leads to ideas.
Ideas generate action.
Action happens one step at a time.
The first step is the most difficult
to determine and to take.

What are the first steps you will take as a result of reading this article?

1. _____
2. _____
3. _____

The Five Things You Absolutely Must Do to Manage Employees Well

Write the Job Description - *Don't "should" all over them.*

If you find yourself saying, "They should know/do..." look at what you have given them in the form of written expectations. This is not just a list of what they currently do given their strengths. It is a list of what you really want them to do, no matter how high those expectations are. And it includes specifics. For example:

Not so Specific: Greet customers and check them in and out.

Specific: Welcome customers with a friendly smile, using their first name. Thank them for coming in and make sure to book their next appointment before they leave.

Coach on the Go - *You need to talk to them!*

This is not just friendly rapport. This is conversation about specific behaviors that you have seen that you like and specific behaviors that you don't like. Having a conversation about their "bad attitude" is not clear enough. It is most often taken as a personal attack, which will shut down communication. They cannot change their behavior to what you expect unless you are clear about the fact that they, for example, "fail to smile at customers and coworkers."

Give your Undivided Attention - *Every one of your direct reports needs some of your undivided attention every month.*

This meeting is not about how you can help them or what they think you or the company could do differently. This is about *them* reporting on their progress and challenges. They come prepared to update you on the status of key projects, metrics, challenges and tasks. They also take notes on the action items they agree to do for next month.

Evaluate their Performance - *Write it down at least once, preferably twice a year.*

Feedback is based on tasks and expectations in the job description and is very specific, citing examples. The employee does a self assessment writing specific examples for the tasks at which they excel and those with which they struggle. Review the results in a meeting where you give them your undivided attention.

Recognize Desired Behavior – *This is much more than "You did a great job today, thanks!"*

Recognize specific behaviors you wish to see repeated. Use both individual and team awards. Be timely and specific. Reward what is important to you and your company. Recognize initiative and achievements. Make recognition fun. Beware of complicated programs that it takes a lot of administration to continue.

Which of these do you do well? Which is most difficult for you?

Reading inspires thought.
Thought leads to ideas.
Ideas generate action.
Action happens one step at a time.
The first step is the most difficult
to determine and to take.

What are the first steps you will take as a result of reading this article?

1. _____
2. _____
3. _____

Insanity

"Doing the same things over and over and expecting different results" is the common definition of insanity and it is attributed to Albert Einstein and Benjamin Franklin. Whoever said it, we are in good company to pay attention to the advice!

We can all look at people who obviously exude insanity and insist on banging their heads against the wall. However, every one of us must look at ourselves and ask: "*What is it* that I am doing over and over and expecting different results?"

We are all a bit insane
We are all a bit insane and I believe we each hold on to something different. But we all, in fact, hold on to something that is not working.

Maybe it's

- a particular activity,

- how you prioritize your tasks,

- your approach to a problem,

- your management style,

- your belief that because you don't need praise, your employees don't either,

- your refusal to write goals,

- your inability to make timely decisions,

- your avoidance of conflict,

- a long term troublesome employee,

- your communication style,

- your tendency to inspire with speeches instead of real conversations,

- a focus on the urgent instead of the important,

- a focus on sales when you really need to fix operations and systems, or

- the way you perceive your and others' potential.

What is it that you are holding on to even though it is not productive for you?

Determine what that is, make a plan, hold yourself accountable, share the plan with someone you trust and have them hold you accountable, and change what needs to be changed in order to get the results you want!

Reading inspires thought.
Thought leads to ideas.
Ideas generate action.
Action happens one step at a time.
The first step is the most difficult
to determine and to take.

What are the first steps you will take as a result of reading this article?

1. _____
2. _____
3. _____

If You Do the Same Things
You Have Always Done

If you do the same things you have always done, you'll get what you've always gotten? Actually you'd be lucky to. Consider the definition of insanity, 'Doing the same things over and over and expecting different results.' This quote is often used to demonstrate the negative consequences of staying in a rut. However, you'd be lucky to achieve even the *same* results doing the same things you've always done. How about the typewriter manufacturer? The economic climate, competitors and your customers' other options change too much to be able to predict even *steady* results by doing the 'tried and true' things you have always done.

Be a Great Learner

Some business principles are constants. However, innovation is essential to business survival. Being talented at anything but being a *great learner* has a limited life span. Just ask the typewriter repairman. You must not cling to what you know and are comfortable with and expect to move forward.

As a leader, you should spend 10 to 20% of your time learning and innovating just to keep from slipping behind. Competitors can copy what you do, but not what you're thinking. How much time do you spend thinking? Innovating? How do you innovate? Read? Research? Talk? Think? Is setting aside *time to think* part of your strategies to reach your goals? Thinking is a completely different activity from 'doing' anything, even doing strategic tasks.

Spend the Time
Have you designated a set time and place to ensure this strategic thinking happens routinely? Do you wonder how much time you need? Schedule an appointment with yourself in your calendar for an hour a week. If that seems like too big a time commitment, start with 15 minutes per week. When you see positive results, you'll find more time until you are at just the right amount of time for you each week. Find a place conducive to learning. Maybe it's the library or the park. Identify how you learn best. Maybe it is at the computer, reading a book, watching a video, or going out and trying something.

If you do the same things you have always done, you'll be lucky to get what you've always gotten. What do you as a leader need to focus on improving? Which article do you really need to read next?

Reading inspires thought.
Thought leads to ideas.
Ideas generate action.
Action happens one step at a time.
The first step is the most difficult
to determine and to take.

What are the first steps you will take as a result of reading this article?

1. _____

2. _____

3. _____

'Management' isn't Evil!
Are you a Leader or a Manager?

With all the popular focus on being a great leader, you may be tempted to believe that being a manager is unnecessary or even bad. You may also be led to believe that everyone can manage operations, but only the very talented can lead people. Neither of these beliefs is true.

Leadership	vs.	Management:
Long-term Vision		Day-to-day function
Doing the right thing		Doing things right
Effectiveness		Efficiency
Innovation		Meeting standards
Sharing power and information		Telling people what they need to know
People and relationships of trust		Structure and systems

The reality is that successful leadership requires a combination of the two and a delicate and sophisticated balance of the vision and the day-to-day action. Different tasks you do, different roles you play, different situations you encounter and different stages of a business life cycle all require differing mixes of wearing these two hats. Both roles are challenging in their own right and you can and should take time to develop the skills it takes to be successful in each.

What parts of your role are in need of the vision of a leader?

What components are hurting for the discipline of a manager?

Delicate Balance

Leading employees is a delicate balance between building relationships and managing the tasks. Some people prefer to connect with employees and build the relationship by learning about employees' goals, what motivates them, and what's important to them, all in order to increase their excitement to be contributing members of the team. Others prefer to set up systems, policies, procedures and structures to ensure what needs to be done, gets done. Which is your preference?

The fact is that both are necessary to turn your employees into excited team members who take initiative to reach company goals and objectives. When you first hire an employee, there is more focus on managing the tasks than building relationships because employees first need to learn what to do. As time goes by and they understand the task, then you can build the relationship in order to activate the person inside.

Where are your employees in the process? Do you keep them in task mode too long? Or do you focus too heavily on the relationship, ignoring the accountability you must provide as the manager in order to get things done?

Reading inspires thought.
Thought leads to ideas.
Ideas generate action.
Action happens one step at a time.
The first step is the most difficult
to determine and to take.

What are the first steps you will take as a result of reading this article?

1. _____
2. _____
3. _____

HOW not IF

The Mechanics of a Conversation

Section Overview

The goal of a conversation is to accomplish something, such as:

- Sharing information

- Making a decision

- Changing behavior

- Setting or clarifying expectations

- Solving a problem

These goals appear easier than they are because, despite best intentions, professionals are not always very good at the mechanics of a conversation.

A common mistake is to assume that in order to ensure the other person is on the same page, that they clearly understand or to get them to agree, you need to talk more. The fact is that people learn, understand, and are open to changing their mind when *they* are talking, not when you are. Articles in this section cover multiple strategies to engage the other person in conversation.

Once the person is talking, then you might run into a smokescreen, a head nod, or an elephant; all of which can impede communication and make your conversations very difficult. It is important to increase your awareness of what might occur and know what to do about it. Maybe there are times in a conversation where you are unsure what to say next. Or you are speaking, but can see that the other person is not listening and they are putting up walls. In these situations, it is time to stop talking and ask some good questions. In the section, "What Do I Say *Now?*" multiple situations are presented with questions that will help you achieve your desired results from tough situations.

Coaching is about developing people over time. Think about it. The coach of a sports team does not give a lecture, tell everyone 'the answers' and then leave! Nor does a coach have one solid conversation and assume their job is done. Coaching requires a lot of "Time Consuming Conversations", requires more than "A Magic Wand," and usually requires more conversation than you think it will as you will read in "The Missing Link."

And every single time you speak, you have a moment, the Opportunity Space™, before you start speaking to decide the very best thing to say and do next. Within this split second, there is enormous opportunity, as there is with each and every word you use, especially "Powerful Words."

Remember to be careful not to assume the conversation itself is the easy part simply because you enjoy people and enjoy talking. Decide not 'If' you will improve your conversations, but 'How' you can change your approach to be more effective.

With the determination to become more effective at the mechanics of a conversation, let's explore 'How,' not 'If' to get it done, one step at a time.

You Can Talk, But Can You Communicate?

Eloquent. Intelligent. Clever. Articulate. It's a pleasure to listen to a well-spoken person.

Communicating, as opposed to speaking, requires that a message is sent *and* that a message is received. Do you ever feel like you are not getting through to someone? You may try to rephrase what you are saying, say it again or remove distractions. These tactics are good speaking tactics, but fail to take into account that in order for the message to be received, the person on the receiving end must be *ready, willing and able* to receive your message.

The ability to hear and understand is often the easiest to ensure. Is the person intelligent, educated on the topic and experienced in the area being discussed? It is the 'ready and willing' that can be missing. Are they worried, upset, offended, personally distracted, colored by their experiences, affected by their successes, their failures, and their interactions with you that have gone well or badly in the past?

You communicate with a variety of people on a variety of topics every day. However, there are key interactions that are difficult and very important. Maybe you:

- are trying to ease tension between two team members.

- are working with a particular person in whom you see great potential.

- are developing leadership skills within your middle managers.

- are trying to decrease turnover in your sales team or front line employees.

- wish to access the creative potential of all your employees to improve your bottom line results through increased efficiency or new product development.

- desire to improve the customer service offered by your organization.

- are trying to wrap up a particularly difficult project.

- must gain cooperation from a key player.

These are most likely the situations where you may wish to spend a bit more time evaluating your effectiveness in communicating. Consider:

- Is your message clear?

- Are you clear about what you wish to accomplish with your communication?

- Have you outlined your points to the extent that someone else can grasp your full message?

- Are you communicating to the right people?

- Are they able to lend their expertise, assistance or suggestions in this area?

- Are you missing any critical individuals?

- Are they ready and willing to listen and respond?

- Where are they coming from?

- What is important to them?

- How do they see the situation?

- What is on their mind *right now?*

To get your message across, the best thing you can do is get the other person talking about it.

What questions can you ask to involve them in conversation so you can listen to how they view the situation, the options and possible solutions? How is this communication making them feel? Worried? Inadequate? Overconfident? Are the two of you communicating or are you talking to a wall? You can do a lot of talking and very little communicating if you aren't asking questions and listening purposefully. Who is it that you find it most difficult to get through to?

Reading inspires thought.
Thought leads to ideas.
Ideas generate action.
Action happens one step at a time.
The first step is the most difficult
to determine and to take.

What are the first steps you will take as a result of reading this article?

1. _____
2. _____
3. _____

Getting People Engaged

Engaged people are those who are interested enough to do something. Engagement requires movement and action.

What makes people act? A desire to act usually comes from a desire to reach something greater than the current position either because of discomfort with the current situation or a vision of what's possible beyond the current reality.

What does that mean for you in trying to get team members, peers, associates, and employees engaged? Create an Invitation and find Common Ground.

Create an Invitation
People act because someone asks them to. Will you help someone who asks? Will you get involved because someone you trust invites you? Will you respond when someone explains what they need you to do?

Too often, people may not get engaged in a process, and in planning, executing and implementing because it is easier not to. It is easier not to put themselves out on a limb, nor extend beyond their level of confidence. They may assume their help or involvement is not needed or assume what they are currently doing is enough. If you see possibility beyond where your team is currently operating, invite others to see what you see, and ask them specifically for their participation.

"You've put a lot of time and effort into this. I appreciate all you've done. I can't help thinking that we could make it even better if we…. Will you help me by …?"

Find Common Ground

People act because there is something in it for them. I don't mean people are self-centered and selfish. I mean that each of us operates from our own point of view and when something is exciting, important and valuable to us, we tend to get involved.

Have you ever learned something new or gained more in-depth knowledge about a cause, a problem or a challenge, and then decided to get (more) involved?

Finding Common Ground requires that you have a conversation with whomever you are trying to get more engaged. It means you share some of your passion, and let them respond and determine for themselves what it is they are excited about. There are often many facets of a project, problem or situation and the specific reason *you* get excited may not be the same reason someone else gets excited. Yet you both become avid workers toward the end goal.

"I was thinking about the reason we started working on this project and how exciting it will be when we achieve the goal of.... What is it that you are most excited about?"

Who on your team needs to be more engaged? Who do you wish would be of more help to you in what you are trying to accomplish? Have you issued the Invitation and do they see the Common Ground?

Reading inspires thought.
Thought leads to ideas.
Ideas generate action.
Action happens one step at a time.
The first step is the most difficult
to determine and to take.

What are the first steps you will take as a result of reading this article?

1. _____
2. _____
3. _____

Why in the World are my Employees doing That?

In order to address the Elephant in the Room you need to have a conversation with the perpetrator(s). The Elephant is something that annoys you or that you find unacceptable, but have not addressed or have not resolved successfully.

The prerequisites to conversation are:

1. *Your genuine curiosity.* If you are simply annoyed and desire the behavior to either stop without your intervention or you want the person gone, you will not be successful in conversation. They must sense that you are genuinely curious and want to help them to improve. Your objective is to connect with them to the point where they are willing to expand their thinking because they trust you.

2. *Your belief in them.* Whether or not history indicates it is true, you must express a belief that the employee can and will improve if you are to connect with them in a conversation enough for them to change or improve. *"I know you can*

do it, " is a very, very powerful and underutilized phrase from a manager or leader's mouth. Say it!

The objective of the conversation is to determine why they are acting the way they are. *You must get them to give you this answer.* You may have a guess, but if you have not been able to fix the problem yet, your guess is probably not the whole picture.

Get Them to Talk

They would love nothing more than to sit there and nod their head in agreement with you. If the problem is a chronic Elephant in the Room, they don't know how to solve it either without this conversation. If they can get away with just nodding their head while you "solve" the problem, they will do so.

1. You might start with, "I'm concerned about the Smith Project which was completed one week after the deadline. What happened?" *Then listen.* They will give you the scenario as they see it.

2. "It's critical we can finish our projects on or before our deadlines. In hindsight, what do you think could have been done differently?" *Wait for them to think and come up with a response.* You can use the brainstorming technique based on the belief that there are always six solutions to every problem. If they have trouble coming up with one, expand their brain and challenge them to come up with six.

3. "Your next big project is the Memphis Project. The deadline is in six weeks. *I believe* that you can figure out a way to make sure it gets done on time. *What is it that you plan to do differently* to ensure that this one is done on or before the deadline?" The definition of insanity is doing the same things over and over and expecting different results. Explain that if they expect their performance to be different, they must identify something specific to do differently.

Elephant in the Room

If they are unwilling to talk and brainstorm with you, then you have an additional Elephant in the Room that needs to be addressed. Then the conversation turns to, "I'm concerned the deadline was missed and I'd like to help you to be more successful. I know you want to do a better job. It doesn't appear that you are willing to talk about it. Help me understand." *Pause and listen.*

Find Something you were not Expecting to Find

If you simply discover the same old reasons for the project being late, you will continue to have the employees who keep 'trying' but nothing seems to improve. Too often, we look for the answer we think is the real reason, the employee is looking for what we want to hear because it will get them off the hot-seat, and both you and the employee walk away "happy" but nothing changes. Continue the curious conversation that keeps them talking until you find a reason for their behavior that you did not expect. This reason forms the basis for ideas of what to do differently.

Having a productive conversation that leads to significantly better performance is one of the hardest things to do. This is often because the manager wants to dominate the conversation to keep it moving. The answer will actually come from the employee who is doing the work and who knows themselves better than you ever could. Talk to them! Connect!

Reading inspires thought.
Thought leads to ideas.
Ideas generate action.
Action happens one step at a time.
The first step is the most difficult
to determine and to take.

What are the first steps you will take as a result of reading this article?

1. _____
2. _____
3. _____

Stop Talking & Get your Point Across

Do you speak more in order to get your point across or to convince someone to do something or think a certain way? Your days are often comprised of conversations where you need to deliver a message, convince someone to see your point, change thought processes or behaviors and in general, get things done and done well!

The challenge is that most people learn best when they are the ones talking, they are given the time and environment in which to think and they are prompted to consider additional points of view.

If you are successful, chances are that you are willing to learn, enjoy gaining new information and are open to new approaches that may further your success. However, you may encounter members of your team who seem resistive to accepting certain new ideas, who put roadblocks in the way of doing things in a new way or who comply, but fail to buy in whole-heartedly to something they've been asked to do.

How do you move past those obstacles to implement new initiatives and bring out the best in each team member in order to benefit from their expertise and abilities?

First, Stop Talking!

First, Stop Talking. Then, ask the right questions to get them talking. If there was a door in front of you that was closed, and you wished to get into the next room, I highly doubt you would keep running into it until it opened! You would use the handle to try to open it. If that didn't work, you might attempt to unlock it. And if that still didn't work, you would look to see what might be jamming the door.

There is a reason why you are not getting the full cooperation and motivation that you desire from another person. You will not find this reason by repeatedly stating your case, explaining why what you desire is so important, educating on the benefits or demanding a change in performance.

I spoke with a manager who told me about something irrational his employees were doing. I asked why he thought they were doing that. He had no idea and had not explored that question. That is not unusual, but it is an obstacle.

Good and Valid Reason

There is a good and valid reason in each person's mind for everything that they do. You may not realize why they are failing to put forth their full participation. It is up to you to ask key questions to determine the roadblock and then work with them to remove it. Try starting with, "I'm concerned about [problem behavior or lack of enthusiasm.] What's happening?"

Asking Questions

In order to facilitate conversation, you might say, "I value your opinion, why do *you* think it happened that way?" or "Help me understand why it played out that way." Continue to explore what really happened until you help them to see the roadblock and why it exists.

Then, you may want to ask, "How else have you seen this task completed successfully?" or "How else could you have approached that situation?" and "This situation arises often, what do you think you could do differently next time to experience a different outcome?"

Action Items

To 'try harder' and 'do better next time' is not enough. Unless you determine why it really happened in the first place (which requires you to be genuinely curious and ask thought provoking questions) there is no reason to believe it won't happen again. In order to do better or try harder, any individual must identify what it is that they *will do differently, no matter how small that change might be.*

If you are getting nowhere with a conversation, tell the employee to take some time to think it through, give them a specific assignment (come up with three things they could do differently, for example) and set an firm appointment time no more than 24 hours later to finish the conversation. They are waiting for you to go away. Don't give up!

These conversations take time, especially to get to the real reason for behavior. Employees will try to give you the answer you want to hear, so you will not make them think through why something really happened or why they are struggling in a particular area. However, if you take the time to remove the roadblock and get to the real reason, you will benefit significantly from improved behavior from that person in the future.

Think about it, if you remove the wedge of wood stuck in the door, you could open it, rather than force it to open and damage the door. Many team members go through life being damaged because they don't have someone who will help them *think and talk* through the challenges they face.

When they are the one talking, they are the one thinking!

Reading inspires thought.
Thought leads to ideas.
Ideas generate action.
Action happens one step at a time.
The first step is the most difficult
to determine and to take.

What are the first steps you will take as a result of reading this article?

1. _____
2. _____
3. _____

Nonverbal Communication - Myth Debunked

There are a lot of messages that a person communicates in addition to the words they say. If you pay attention, their body language can be a significant source of information.

However, if you'd really like to have the master list of all the possible nonverbal body language signs (eye contact, crossed arms, slouching) and what they mean, I'm afraid you're out of luck. Most 'answers' and generalizations are just not true all the time.

Possibilities

People act differently and communicate differently based on a lot of things, not only what they are feeling at the moment. There is reliable information available about nonverbal signals, there is just *not one list* of the 'right' answers that apply to every person in every situation. Here are a few examples:

1. Lack of eye contact means they are lying. Well, the amount and nature of eye contact can be telling, but the exact moment it breaks may not be significant.

2. Folding arms means defensiveness. Maybe. Or maybe they are getting comfortable, or thinking, or relaxed. I've personally seen them all, and done them all.

3. 'That tone' means they are annoyed. Tone of voice is not the same for everyone. Some people use tone to their advantage. Others purposely avoid changes in tone and pitch. Others have their natural tone that follows them everywhere.

4. Squaring up to you means they are becoming aggressive. Maybe they are increasingly interested.

5. Turning feet and shoulders away from you means they are disinterested. Maybe they are just getting comfortable.

6. Their head nod means they are in complete agreement. I've always said that when a person nods, it may very well mean nothing. They may be just trying to get you to stop talking because you believe they agree. They may want you to stop talking because they are confused, bored, uninterested, or have other priorities at the moment. A nod can also indicate agreement, politeness, "Go away!", or "I get it!"

7. Closed hands means they are withholding information. Maybe they just naturally sit that way or are thinking about something totally different than your current conversation.

8. Leaning forward means aggressiveness. Or maybe they are excited and interested.

9. Leaning back means they are thinking deeply about something you said. Or it could mean they are disengaged.

Keep in mind that you can think about four times faster than someone naturally speaks. That is why it is so hard to listen. Your brain has so much excess capacity. Therefore, when you are speaking to someone, what they do nonverbally may or may not be directly related to the current conversation.

Patterns
What can nonverbal communication tell you? Most importantly, nonverbal communication patterns must be learned and changes observed.

What are the common patterns for the people with whom you are communicating? What makes them change? How do they hold themselves most of the time? How do they feel most of the time?

1. Are they often nervous and defensive? Then a change in body language may mean you are relieving their stress and opening a dialog. That's a good thing.

2. Are they often participative and productive? A change in body language may mean you have said or done something that has closed the conversation and you have lost their buy-in. That needs to be addressed.

Determine what triggers someone to change tone, posture, eye contact and movements and decide if that change is a good thing. Then, you can adjust your communication in the moment based on their body language and achieve your desired results from the conversation.

And, by the way, words are important too, so brush up on your listening skills, and spend more than 25% of your energy listening to the words in order to gain insight on the entire communication message that the other person is sending!

Reading inspires thought.
Thought leads to ideas.
Ideas generate action.
Action happens one step at a time.
The first step is the most difficult
to determine and to take.

What are the first steps you will take as a result of reading this article?

1. _____
2. _____
3. _____

Smokescreens

Unacceptable behavior is unacceptable behavior. Period.
So treat it as such.

Too often managers fail to address a problem behavior and fail to hold the employee accountable. Instead, the employee presents a reason for their behavior which acts as a smokescreen. The reason becomes the point of your discussion with the employee instead of talking about their inappropriate behavior.

Reasons are real and there are always reasons the employee will present for their unacceptable behavior. And you may forgive an incident because of the reason, but you must still have the conversation about the behavior being unacceptable, and that it must not happen again. If the behavior goes unaddressed and the reason is simply discussed, this may lead to a pattern of repeated unacceptable behavior.

Example:
Employee is rude to a customer.
Supervisor (pulls employee aside): "I'm concerned about the way you treated Mrs. Smith this morning."

Employee: "I'm so overwhelmed, we have a ton of things due today, and Bob isn't helping me."
(Warning - Smokescreen)

The smokescreen works:
Supervisor: "Bob's not helping you? Why not?"

Employee: "He has that other project he's working on, but I can't do this alone. He needs to be spending some time here with the customers too. When I talked to him, he just gave me an attitude."

And on and on, the discussion of Bob - the reason and the smokescreen - continues and the unacceptable behavior goes unaddressed. The employee's concern may be valid and the problem with Bob may need to be addressed, but the employee must also be held accountable for treating a customer rudely.

Example:
Employee is rude to a customer.
Supervisor (pulls employee aside): "I'm concerned about the way you treated Mrs. Smith this morning."

Employee: "I'm so overwhelmed, we have a ton of things due today, and Bob isn't helping me."
(Warning - Smokescreen)

The smokescreen does not work:
Supervisor: "Whew, it seems like you are quite frustrated at the moment. I'd like to help you work through that. First, we need to take just a moment to talk about what happened with Mrs. Smith."

Employee: "Well, she was being really demanding about what we promised we would deliver to her by yesterday. I told her it was only a day late and that I was really busy."

Supervisor: "It sounds like we dropped the ball. Our customers are the reason we're successful, and we need to treat them really well. It's very important we meet deadlines, treat them with respect, apologize when necessary and not burden them with any of our internal problems. How do you think you could have handled that situation differently?"

When are you failing to address inappropriate behaviors or accepting smokescreens?

Reading inspires thought.
Thought leads to ideas.
Ideas generate action.
Action happens one step at a time.
**The first step is the most difficult
to determine and to take.**

What are the first steps you will take as a result of reading this article?

1. _____
2. _____
3. _____

A Nod of the Head Means...

You're prepared to explain something that is really important. You've done the research and assembled the important details. You are certain that your explanation will lead your employee to get excited and focused, and to take initiative to get things started.

As you explain, the employee nods their head, sometimes in a small subtle nod, and other times more like a bobble-head doll on a bumpy car ride. As you summarize your key points, the employee nods and says, "Okay."

What does this mean?

N O T H I N G!

Unless the employee engages in conversation, they probably have understood very little.

Therefore, if you want the employees to get excited and engaged, you must get them talking! First, share some of your big picture thoughts and ask them an open-ended question like:

- What is most interesting to you about this idea?

- How do you see yourself becoming involved in this project?

Then share details about the initiative and ask other open-ended questions like:

- What about this is most exciting to you?

- I can definitely see you playing an important role in Project A. How do you think we should get started?

- I'd like some suggestions from you about Project A. If you don't have any immediate thoughts, why don't you bring three suggested approaches to our meeting on Thursday?

Most people believe that they can improve how well they are understood by talking more. Exactly the opposite is true. A person understands much more completely when they are talking, which requires them to do some thinking.

When you want the employee to act purposefully, get them to think first. In order to get them to think, give them direction and get them talking.

Reading inspires thought.
Thought leads to ideas.
Ideas generate action.
Action happens one step at a time.
The first step is the most difficult
to determine and to take.

What are the first steps you will take as a result of reading this article?

1. _____
2. _____
3. _____

The Elephant in the Room.
Be Careful! He'll Squash You!

What is it in your work environment that annoys you or that you find unacceptable, which you have not addressed or have not resolved successfully?

Typically, each person has their own levels of tolerance for different situations and the behaviors of others. Combined with their comfort zone, this determines what they are willing to actually address.

Have you worked with:

1. Whiners?

2. Absolute minimum performers?

3. Missed deadlines but not by much?

4. Chronic poor performance in one area, with a million excuses?

5. Unspoken tension?

6. Give an inch, we'll take a mile?

Have you tried to address situations such as these? Maybe you have resolved some of these situations well, but you probably tolerate other situations, although grudgingly, because you're not quite sure what to do.

The Elephant

Think about yourself in a conference room that seats eight people. Now add a full size elephant. It would be crowded, difficult to communicate, a bit intimidating and probably downright uncomfortable at times. Pretty similar to the feelings people experience when one of the problems listed on the previous page stays unresolved, especially for any significant period of time.

The first step is to name the elephant. Think about yourself in the same room above with a blindfold on. It gets stuffy in the room, you keep walking into a 'wall' and there is no space, you get hit by a trunk every now and then and it doesn't smell so pleasant. You must name the problem that exists in order to change it. Look beyond the obvious. Look for the root of the problem. Look deeper than you may think necessary.

Then, decide to have a conversation about it. Don't dance around the problem. Talk to the person. Connect with them and try to understand where they are coming from and why in the world they are acting the way they are. Then, come up with what can be done differently to change the situation.

Reading inspires thought.
Thought leads to ideas.
Ideas generate action.
Action happens one step at a time.
The first step is the most difficult
to determine and to take.

What are the first steps you will take as a result of reading this article?

1. _____
2. _____
3. _____

Addressing the Elephant – Scenarios

The Elephant: Missed Deadlines

The elephant is the huge problem (they frequently miss task deadlines) that is preventing you from being able to successfully address the problem at hand (one missed deadline).

Speak in a way that demonstrates your determination and your belief that they will resolve these situations successfully. Ask all questions with genuine curiosity.

I noticed that Task A was not completed by the deadline. What happened?

Employee: Excuse, excuse
I'd like to hear your plan to complete Task A and to communicate with the stakeholder. Before we have that discussion, I'd like to discuss a situation that seems to be recurring.

Not only did Task A not get done by today, Task B did not get done by the deadline earlier this week, Task C did not get done by a deadline last week and Task D was a month late.

Let them speak, and then continue.
When you and I have spoken about these past due tasks, you tend to mention the fires that have arisen and the obstacles that others' have created. Knowing that fires will arise and you will need to effectively communicate with, and rely on, others to get your job done well, I'd like to discuss what you will do differently in order to complete your tasks by deadlines, despite these realities.

Let them speak, and then continue.
Each of these deadlines is a real deadline that exists to meet the needs of our customers, and is not moveable. When we miss it, there are tangible negative consequences for our customers.

Explore all variables:
- What types of tasks do you find you have the most difficulty in completing?

- You have agreed to the deadlines. Can you explain how you determine your plan to meet deadlines before you agree?

- Share with me how you prioritize your week. Your day?

- What are the most common 'fires' that pull you off task?

  o Are you the best person to address those fires?

○ How do you determine if they need to be addressed immediately?

The Elephant: Tossing the Monkey on to your Back

What you'll hear: "I'm just not good at that." or "I hate doing reports."

Ask all questions with genuine curiosity.
Let's talk about that for just a minute. Typically, when I hear someone say, "I hate doing reports," they don't see any reason for doing them. Tell me what makes *you* say you hate them.

Employee speaks.
What is it specifically that you hate about reports?

When you say "they are too long," share with me what you think *should* be on the report.

What information do you think we should gather?

What business decisions do you think we could make better or faster with that information?

What ideas do you have for gathering and communicating [business information]?

Reading inspires thought.
Thought leads to ideas.
Ideas generate action.
Action happens one step at a time.
The first step is the most difficult
to determine and to take.

What are the first steps you will take as a result of reading this article?

1. _____
2. _____
3. _____

Turning "Yeah, buts…." into "A-ha's!"

Does it drive you crazy when you have a good idea, an original approach or a unique solution and the first thing someone can say is, "Yeah, but…."? It's time to take those words and turn them into "Yes, and…."

Before we jump ahead, those who routinely offer the, "Yeah, but…." are probably the individuals who ground those of us with wild, crazy and risky ideas. So, it can be a good balance. Their caution may be for good reason and they may bring up valid points of view.

The "Yeah, but…."
First, open your mind to listen to the objection and *ask a clarifying question or two.* When they say, "Yeah, but what happens when the customer says 'No'?" you might respond with, "Let's look at that for a moment. Which customers do you think would most likely respond that way?" and "What is it, do you think, that would make them feel that way?" Productive conversation will follow.

Then, *address the negativity elephant.* The elephant is the problem or roadblock that is preventing the conversation from continuing in a positive direction in order to explore possibilities. "I hear your concern, *and* it's good to hear why you feel that way. Now, I'd like to continue exploring my idea a bit more. Let's start by looking at the benefits of what's been suggested." Continue with conversation about possibilities.

Too often, a "Yeah, but..." ends productive discussion because the person who brought up the idea feels shot down, may not continue and may get defensive. The "Yeah, but..." team member who brought up the objection gets defensive in return. Each person gets stuck defending themselves because they haven't been given any credibility and have not been able to explore their concern.

The "A-ha!"

When the clarifying questions are asked, the elephant addressed and the original idea explored, both people are more open to the discussion and good things happen. With every team member engaged in productive conversation, you are on your way to an "A-ha!" such as, "A-ha! I've never thought of it that way! The idea may only apply to the top 20% of our customers, but those are the ones who we'd like to duplicate. My concern was valid that we'd lose some customers, but if we lose some of the bottom 15%, that may be worth the trade off! I'm glad we had this discussion. Let's do it!"

Reading inspires thought.
Thought leads to ideas.
Ideas generate action.
Action happens one step at a time.
The first step is the most difficult
to determine and to take.

What are the first steps you will take as a result of reading this article?

1. _____

2. _____

3. _____

The Coaching Conversation

Coaching is having a series of conversations with an individual in order to help them access their hidden potential to achieve greater levels of success.

It is essential that you have both 'Conversations on the Go' as well as 'Undivided Attention Meetings' in order to coach your employees effectively. When you see desired or unacceptable behaviors, sometimes you need to address them immediately for greatest impact. Other times you need to focus the employee on their improvement in a planned meeting where you have each other's undivided attention. In which meeting you bring up an issue depends on the urgency of the needed change in behavior. If you wait and an unacceptable behavior continues, your frustration increases as does the employee's resistance to change. This makes the conversation more difficult when it does occur.

Conversations on the Go
Brief coaching conversations that occur on the spot.

1. You bring up the desired behavior. "I'm excited about how you [specific behavior] because [why

it is important to company/goals/vision]." Pause and listen.

2. Or you bring up the unacceptable behavior and get them talking. "I'm concerned about… because…. What Happened?" Ask a few clarifying questions.

   a. Then you talk. Explain current unacceptable behaviors, describing them specifically. "Your bad attitude" and "your lack of initiative" are not specific behaviors.

   b. Get commitment to precise, doable action from the employee.

   c. Determine a follow-up date. It may be during your monthly meeting with them.

Undivided Attention Meetings
Monthly meeting where each of your direct reports prepares for and attends a meeting with you.

**This is not about how you can help them or what they think you or the company could do differently.
This is about the employee reporting on their progress and challenges.**

According to a set agenda communicated prior to the meeting:

1. They report their successes and progress first, according to goals you have set.

2. They report on set metrics, projects, and status.

3. They identify the areas where they have fallen short and what they will *do differently.*

4. You compliment them on successes and progress you've seen.

5. You comment on their performance that can be improved, using specific examples of unacceptable and acceptable behaviors.

6. *Get commitment to precise, measurable and achievable action.* Assist them to identify action items and strategies. This is not easy and may take time. Engage in discussion to pinpoint specific action items that will impact their performance. Use clarifying questions like, "Can you give me an example?" and "Can you be more specific?" and "What have you tried in the past?" Watch for smokescreens and tangents.

7. Determine a follow-up date and set a follow-up meeting appointment on the calendar with an agreed upon agenda.

The only way you can help your team to access their potential and move to a higher level of performance is if you coach them. Even the best employees need your coaching. Michael Jordan had a coach!

Reading inspires thought.
Thought leads to ideas.
Ideas generate action.
Action happens one step at a time.
The first step is the most difficult
to determine and to take.

What are the first steps you will take as a result of reading this article?

1. _____
2. _____
3. _____

Time Consuming Conversations
Waste of Time or Absolute Best Use of Your Time?

One of the biggest time wasters in your business day is time spent talking with other people!
and
One of the absolute best uses of your work time is productive conversation with people important to your success!

What is the difference? Working productively with the right group of people is the key to multiplying success. However, people often fear something new, wish to preserve their self-image and self-confidence, and don't always get to the point in a conversation. Therefore, if you wish for your 'people time' to be productive, it must be done purposefully.

Schedule appointments to talk.
If you plan to meet with another person and have a conversation, do it purposefully. If you just 'stop by' their office or give them a call without a plan, you may end up wasting their time and yours. And they may do the same with you.

Set expectations ahead of time.

When you need to talk to someone, plan a time and day and have an agenda. Set a time and date on your calendars, even 15 minutes from now, to give each person time to move through their initial reaction to the issue or problem, and to prepare for the meeting. Have the conversation about the agenda ahead of time: "When we speak, I will... and you will... in order to accomplish [goal, task or decision]." This works both up *and* down the chain of command.

For example, "I'd like to talk to you about the production logs. How about Tuesday at 1:00pm for 30 minutes? Before then, I will review the log for my areas of concern. And you could review the log compared to last month's as well as looking for overall opportunities for improvement. When we sit down, we'll go though the last two months, each sharing our observations. Does that work for you?" Make sure you secure their commitment to the agenda you suggest. If they don't agree, edit or change it so that you can both prepare appropriately and not argue about the agenda during the meeting.

If someone approaches you and wants to talk immediately, tell them you are right in the middle of something, want to be able to give them your full concentration, and are wondering if you could meet with them in 20 minutes. Then, ascertain from them what it is they need from you when you meet. This requires them to think through the results they desire (which they may not have done yet), and allows you to prepare as well, saving both of you time and potential frustration.

Improve your ability to ask good questions.
In these conversations, you want to remain in control, specifically of making sure something productive results from the conversation. Gladly take that responsibility. In order to do that, you need to ask questions from the standpoint of genuine curiosity to determine where they are coming from and how that relates to what you are trying to accomplish. With the information you gather, you can then notice excuses, frustrations in the form of roadblocks, and cries for attention that can be in the way of productive discussion.

When *you* talk, you share information. You rarely can change anyone's mind by talking. By asking curious questions, you encourage the other person to talk. When *they* talk, you hear how they are thinking. When they talk, you can prompt them to consider your point of view, and help them to reach a conclusion, considering what you value. When they talk is when they think through things and may change their mind as a result.

Work to understand the other person.
The difficulty with having a conversation is that it is with a person who has their own feelings, experiences, biases and expectations. The first thing they say is rarely the whole picture – as it is for you. Ask your questions. Give them time.

Schedule a follow-up conversation if it is important to them or to you.

Set a time, date, and agenda for that conversation and commit to making it happen.

Reading inspires thought.
Thought leads to ideas.
Ideas generate action.
Action happens one step at a time.
The first step is the most difficult
to determine and to take.

What are the first steps you will take as a result of reading this article?

1. _____
2. _____
3. _____

A Magic Wand

Do you ever wish for a magic wand to be able to vaporize a particular individual or two who works for you?

You need to get rid of negative, toxic and aggravating people who are not the right fit for their job. Many managers hold on to someone too long for fear of firing them, or because of a desire to avoid the uncomfortable and difficult nature of a termination.

However, the aggravating people are not always 'toxic' or a bad fit for the job, sometimes they just require management and leadership that is both challenging and requires a time commitment.

Many leaders do not have the ability or the desire to spend the time and energy to bring out the best in someone and help them to access their potential.

Developing people may be a great cause of stress to you and it may seem easier to vaporize the employee with the magic wand. On the other hand, the best employees in a company are usually one of two types:

1. As soon as they were interviewed, the leader knew they had found a gem, and the employee has been a top performer ever since.

2. They were mediocre employees to start, probably frustrating in some areas, but someone took the time to coach them to become the star employees they are today.

Beyond the few star employees, we most often have teams of people who do a good job (and are sometimes aggravating), but certainly not the great job of which they are capable!

Coaching to develop an employee must include:

- Setting goals with them.

- Helping them to identify workable strategies.

- Holding them accountable to determining the first and next steps toward enacting those strategies.

- Creating a situation where *they* take responsibility and initiative to report on their successes and challenges and determine what they will do differently to make progress.

This coaching requires the leader to continue to 'force' the employee to realize the success of which they are capable. 'Forcing' the employee means that the manager is doggedly holding them accountable. 'The success of which they are capable' means that the employee is doing their part to achieve the potential the manager sees that they themselves have not yet seen or acknowledged. *Don't give up when you have a team of good employees when you could have a team of great employees!*

Reading inspires thought.
Thought leads to ideas.
Ideas generate action.
Action happens one step at a time.
The first step is the most difficult
to determine and to take.

What are the first steps you will take as a result of reading this article?

1. _____
2. _____
3. _____

The 'Missing Link' Conversation

As a leader, your role is often that of a problem-solver, fire extinguisher, expert advisor, jack-of-all-trades juggler. When you do 'solve' a problem, what do you do to take care of the people involved?

This may seem like an odd question. Once their problem is solved, you have taken care of them, have you not?

A couple things to remember:

- The first problem someone brings you is rarely the real problem. It may be a symptom, a cry for attention, or a smokescreen to shield a problem they would prefer you did not discover.

- Members of your team, given their knowledge and expertise, are probably fairly capable of solving most technical or logistical problems themselves. It is usually the mental roadblocks, professional obstacles, difficult relationships and resistance to change they may experience which may be the real problem behind the problem.

One More Conversation

Therefore, as their leader, when you think you are done, have one more conversation. When they say that all is well, you may want to acknowledge your appreciation for their efforts, let them know how much their insight is needed and plan a conversation in a week to touch base on progress. This conversation should be put on the calendar. The agenda is established where they will report on their progress, not wait for you to quiz them at that time.

This additional conversation achieves two things:

1. It creates a situation where they expect accountability to happen and therefore carry out their tasks in a way that they would be proud to report accomplishments a week later.

2. Allows them the time to have frustrations surface, acknowledge challenges they may be facing and know they have an avenue through which to voice those concerns.

Simply putting a bandaid on the problem that existed, without treating the wound underneath, would only make it resurface in a more ugly way later. This would require double your time, and confuse you when you think that you, as the knowledgeable leader, have solved the problem once already. *This may also lead you to the conclusion, that no matter how many times you 'solve' your team's problems, they can't get it right.* The fact is that you are missing a piece of the real problem, the people piece, and that is what is making the problem recur.

Do you spend time on the 'people piece' of problems?

Reading inspires thought.
Thought leads to ideas.
Ideas generate action.
Action happens one step at a time.
The first step is the most difficult
to determine and to take.

What are the first steps you will take as a result of reading this article?

1. _____

2. _____

3. _____

Seize the Opportunity

Do you ever feel out of control? Often the *only* part of a situation that you can control is your reaction to it. There are those critical seconds between what someone else says or does and your response. In this *Opportunity Space*™, you have the opportunity to make the very most out of each and every situation.

People will say and do things you don't like, don't respect and don't understand. You have expectations for what others will do, what they will accomplish and how they will present themselves.

I am sure you have been tempted to say, "What do you mean by that? That's totally wrong! How can you think like that?" However, if this person brought you a suggestion or idea and you respond this way, your chance of *ever* hearing another idea or seeing any initiative from this person is very slim. Every word that comes out of your mouth has an enormous impact either immediately or in the future.

The Opportunity

You have the opportunity to make every interaction the best it can be. Taking advantage of the *Opportunity Space*™ by carefully responding will prove very valuable. First, approach what they say with a grain of salt. Ask yourself, "Why are they saying or doing these things?" Understanding their motives, no matter how different than yours, will help you make the most of the situation. Then ask yourself, "What do I really want to accomplish now and in the long term?" and "What can I do or say *right now* that will help me to accomplish my goals now and in the long term?"

You cannot win every battle, so don't choose to fight every one. Employees won't follow every policy, procedure and instruction they are given. It is critical that you decide which rules are important to enforce and discuss now, and which infractions can be corrected in the long term.

Seizing those crucial seconds and taking advantage of that *Opportunity Space*™ will lead to more successful interactions and long term success with your employees as well as everyone else with whom you interact. Talk about making the most of your time! The way you choose to use even those few seconds can have an enormous impact on your business results!

The Three Questions

In the *Opportunity Space*™, stop and ask yourself The Three Questions:

1. What do I really want to accomplish?

2. Where are they coming from?

3. How am I making them feel?

Let's look at those three questions in more detail.

What do I really want to accomplish?

This requires you to think long term, not only about what would make you feel good in the moment (such as proving you are right). If you can visualize great potential in those with whom you interact, you will treat them in a way that in the long term will help them to reach that potential.

The first step in solving problems is to define the problem. That may not be as easy as it appears. Quality gurus will tell you to ask, "Why?" until you find the root cause of the problem. So, what happens when the problem is not based on logic? What if it is based on people, who by nature are emotional beings?

Then, ask yourself, "What do I really want to accomplish in the long term?" *(be it a week, a month or a year),* not simply, "How can I get through this challenge in front of me?" For example, if you want future cooperation, proving someone else wrong, even if they are, will not bring you closer to what you want to accomplish in the long run. Logically, they are incorrect. Emotionally, they prefer not to admit it. If it is not a serious mistake, preserve the relationship, let them off easy and find a solution together.

Think of a challenge you are currently facing: Are you missing or avoiding the illogical factors driven by emotion?

Where are they coming from?
Each person has a lifetime of experiences that determine how they see the world, no matter how young they are. These are extremely real to each person, even if they don't make sense to anyone else.

You may believe that the majority of challenges, especially in a business arena, can be addressed with logical strategies. However, leaders are often faced with the reality that people act more frequently based on emotion than logic.

Next time logic does not appear to explain the situation, consider the people involved and ask yourself the question, "Where are they coming from?" You will be pleasantly surprised at the richness inherent in the enormous variety and depth of histories, beliefs, values and viewpoints.

Next time someone does something that makes you want to scream and wonder, "Now *why* did they do that?" get curious! If you let yourself be mad at the person, they will become resistive. If you ignore the problem, you will bottle the frustration. If you wait to address the issue, they will become defensive when you do confront them in the future. Consider being honestly curious as to why they did what they did.

In response to the proclamation, "I should not need to baby-sit my employees – they are acting like children!" I often answer, "They are not acting like children.

They are acting like people." People are different, sometimes strange, motivated by numerous different things, acting based on their beliefs and past experiences, and responding to what they thought you said.

As an authentically curious leader, investigate the situation with the other person: "Tell me what happened. Can you explain what you were thinking about? How did you come to that conclusion?" Listen with an open mind for their answers in order to seize the opportunity to learn more about a key member of your team, tweak your expectations of their performance and build a stronger relationship with that person.

Are you genuinely curious? Or just annoyed when something goes wrong?

How am I making them feel?

People are emotional beings. People make decisions emotionally, they only rationalize them logically. How a person feels will determine how they act. Imagine how you are making the other person feel by what you do and say. Feelings just happen. What a person can control is what they do as a result of how they feel. Their behavior is what you are trying to influence by positively affecting how you impact what they are feeling.

Applied consistently and completely, The Three Questions produce dramatically positive results in conversations.

Why do they work? Because you will bring out the best in others when you interact in a way that makes them feel good about themselves. People will maximize their potential when they are confident, even if they are outside their comfort zone and learning something new. As a leader, you can create the environment through your interactions with others where they feel good enough about themselves to learn, to grow, to take initiative and to push themselves to the next level.

The Three Questions apply to every conversation, from the cashier at the grocery store to deep conversations with your spouse or best friend. Yes, you can maximize productivity and employee motivation by applying these questions before you speak or act, and you can also make an enormous difference in the lives of those whom you care about.

Reading inspires thought.
Thought leads to ideas.
Ideas generate action.
Action happens one step at a time.
The first step is the most difficult
to determine and to take.

What are the first steps you will take as a result of reading this article?

1. _____
2. _____
3. _____

Powerful Words in Difficult Conversations

Have you ever seen the person with whom you were speaking either 'light up' or 'shut down' in reaction to something you said? The words you choose can make a huge difference.

Be aware of these powerful words and use them carefully and purposefully:

No – "No" stops people in their tracks. It puts up a wall. It closes down communication. Even if you disagree or feel the answer is "No," you can sometimes still answer "Yes" and clarify the conditions in your response.

For example, the employee asks, "Can I have a $10/hour raise?" You could say, "No way!" Or you could say, "I'm glad to see your drive. Here's what I would need to see in order to give you a raise of that size. You would need to increase your production by 200%, train new people in the position and be a leader on our annual project."

Yes – At the same time, "Yes" is extremely powerful. It makes people happy to talk to you. It opens doors. It opens communication. If there is any way you can be honest and forthright and say "Yes," do so.

For example, "Yes, I'd be happy to look at that. Let's find 10 minutes next week," is much better than saying, "I'm too busy and can't look at that right now." That would cause them to feel unimportant, no matter how busy they know you are.

You – It's almost impossible to start a directive sentence with the word "You" without it feeling like you are pointing a finger.

An example: "You need to fix that problem." Instead you might say, "I'd like to see you take on that challenge. Why don't you give it a try and if you're struggling come see me to ask me some questions."

Why – "Why" can be a pushy sort of word, even if you don't mean it to come across that way.

An example: If I asked you, "Where did you go to college?" You tell me where, and I ask, "Why?" You say, "Because I liked it there when I visited." I say, "Why?" Eventually, you start to feel as if I am being critical of your decisions. Use the other "W" words if at all possible to ask the same question, but in a less pushy way. "What made you decide to attend that college?" "When did you make a decision on which college to attend?" "Where else did you consider attending?"

But – When you put "but" in the middle of a sentence, you are usually saying that one half of the sentence is a lie.

An example: "I really like that idea, but it won't work." "That's a great idea, but…" is essentially saying that it is not a good idea. Replace the "but" with a pause or an "and." "That's a great idea, and I'd like to explore the details a bit more, including the cost of implementation."

Their name – Everyone likes the sound of their own name. Take a moment to realize how little you say the names of those with whom you spend the most time. You tend to just talk if you are around someone a lot. Getting someone's attention by using their name is powerful and will start the conversation on a positive note.

Have you ever responded powerfully to one of these words? Maybe you bristled when someone told you "No!" or started a statement with the word "You." On the other hand, maybe you felt good when you heard the word, "Yes," or someone used your name when they were speaking with you. Do you use these powerful words often and well?

Reading inspires thought.
Thought leads to ideas.
Ideas generate action.
Action happens one step at a time.
The first step is the most difficult
to determine and to take.

What are the first steps you will take as a result of reading this article?

1. _____

2. _____

3. _____

What Do I Say Now?

Any Problem Clarifying Questions

All questions are phrased generically so that you can insert your situation-specific information.

Ask all questions with genuine curiosity.
Can you give me an example?
Can you tell me more about that?
Can you be more specific?
What do you think is causing that to happen?
Can you tell me what you mean by, "Done?"
How long has this been happening?
What specifically do you mean?
Who else is involved?
Who were you hoping would do that?
Where exactly is the problem?
When did that problem start?
By how much?
What have you tried in the past?
How is this affecting you?
How frustrated are you, on a scale of one to ten?
Really? What do you think is keeping you from being more productive?

What about this is most important to you?
When will you consider this completely finished?
What else do you need to learn to be more successful?
What does that mean?
How did you reach that conclusion?
Can you share some examples?
To what extent does that saying apply here?
What do you really mean?
Can you clarify that for me?
How does that statement apply to....?
What are the implications of that statement?
What do you conclude from that information and what is occurring?
Is there anything else of which I need to be aware?
What are you hoping I will do?
What happened?
What can you do differently?

Employee Complaint

You are curious and genuinely interested in tone and speech. You wait for their answers, and avoid appearing defensive.

Ask all questions with genuine curiosity.
Tell me what happened.
How did this impact you?
How did you become involved?
Has this happened before?
Have you brought this to your manager in the past?
What did you do?
Have you talked to [person complaining about]?
What did they say?
What are you hoping I can do?

What made you bring it to me?
What do you want to happen?
What can you do to improve the situation?
How do you think they would describe the situation?
Why do you really think they did what they did?

Thank you for bringing this to my attention. I will look into it further. For now, I will…[your action items] and you will…[their action items]. Let's touch base again in [time frame/set appointment on calendar].

Task Incomplete

Ask all questions with genuine curiosity.
I'm concerned that [task] did not get done, what happened?
Employee speaks.
By when did you agree to have it done?
What steps did you take?
At what point did you get stuck?
What made you feel stuck?
What did you do then?
In hindsight, how might you have approached it differently?
What are the first steps you will take today?
What will you do differently this time?
Who do you need to speak to about the adjusted timeframe?
At what point will you seek assistance?

They're Wrong!

Ask all questions with genuine curiosity.

I did not get that same impression from the conversation. Can you share what led you to that conclusion?
Tell me a little bit more about how you see that playing out.
Can you tell me what happened this morning?
I'm concerned about… What happened?
I might be missing something. Here's how I see it…
I am hearing that there is some disagreement between you and [team member], what's going on?
Follow up with applicable "Any Problem Clarifying Questions."

Commitment to Mission

Mission components may include objectives such as on time delivery or anticipating customer needs.

Ask all questions with genuine curiosity.
I'd like to talk to you about [specific mission component, vision component, objective]. Where do you think we are on a scale of 1 to 10 with ten being the very best that we could ever be?
Do you really think we are a ten? You believe we are the best we could ever be and there is no room to improve? What does a five look like? What does a 15 look like?
How do you think we are currently positively affecting our [stakeholders/customers/peers/internal customers]?
Since we are not a ten, how do you think we are currently negatively affecting our [stakeholders/customers/peers/internal customers]?
What would it take for us to become a ten in this area?

What specifically can *you* do on a daily basis to bring us closer to a 10?

Where can you team up with fellow employees to improve [component]?

On a scale of 1 to 10, how excited are you about [component]?

On a scale of 1 to 10, how committed are you to [component]?

This [component] is critical to who we are and what we are trying to accomplish. Without it, we are simply mediocre and that is unacceptable to me and to [boss] and to you, I'm sure. What do you need to learn in order to be able to contribute more to [component]?

Avoiding Responsibility

Ask all questions with genuine curiosity.
Example: They say, "I'm just no good at handling angry customers."

It sounds as though you have a concern about your ability to handle angry customers. Can you share a bit more about that with me?

Can you give me a specific example of a time that did not go well?

With whom do you feel comfortable working?

Tell me about a time when you were able to successfully deal with an angry customer? Can you share an example with me?

Who do you know who is really good at those situations? What do you think it would take for you to become more skilled in this area?

Let's talk about "how" you can improve your skills in this area, and not "if" this should be part of your job.

What are the most common challenges that come your way [in this area]?

Which part of this do you feel is your responsibility?

What is the best way to approach these situations?

Whose responsibility is it to handle these angry customers now?

I have made some suggestions about how to approach this. Share with me what happened when you tried one of those approaches. How have they worked for you?

Can you share how you think this is best approached?

About how much time do you spend on this? Where do you find yourself spending more of your time?

What has been your experience when you do stick your neck out to handle a difficult customer?

What has been the customer response when you have spoken to an angry person in the past?

Do you feel it is an option to not address these situations?

What's the worst that can happen if you take on this role?

What's the best that can happen if you take on this role?

What is your biggest obstacle to improving in this area?

If you don't do it, who do you think should be responsible?

How do you feel when you prepare to address a customer issue?

Defensive

Ask all questions with genuine curiosity.
They say, "Well, you [Mr. Supervisor] did this...."

Maybe I did miss something. Let's talk through this so we don't run into this situation again. Can you share what you expected me to do?

Help me to understand why you see that as my role.

What skills/abilities do you need to develop to be able to take on that task yourself?

What specifically did you agree to do?

How did that go?

I'd like you to take responsibility for [task they are putting on you]. What would it take for that to happen?

What steps are you going to take from here?

Excuses

Ask all questions with genuine curiosity.

They say, "I didn't get that done because…."

Tell me more about that.

How did it [the distraction] come up?

What made you choose to do [excuse] instead of what you agreed to do?

How else could you have approached [excuse]?

Are you the best person to handle that?

Should you be the first person that people come to or is it more appropriate for you to be the backup person?

Who else could you train to handle this task?

When will you have that completed by?

Did that [excuse] require your expertise?

If you didn't step in, what do you think would have happened?

Is there any chance that you welcomed that distraction?

Were you stuck at that point on the [project/task at hand]?

Did you come right back to the [project/task at hand]?

What could you do to both stay on track *and* support your team members?

Has this ever happened to you before?

With your expertise, I would expect that you would see this coming, what happened?

They Don't Want to be in the Conversation

Ask all questions with genuine curiosity.

I'm getting the impression that you'd prefer not to have this discussion. Is that correct?

What are you hoping to get out of our conversation?

Typically, people walk into a discussion hoping certain things would be discussed. What is it for you that you really want to talk about?

What is one thing you are hoping I won't bring up? Why is that?

What are you sick of re-hashing?

What is it that is most important to you about [current objective]?

Which of your goals is most exciting to you?

On which goal do you think you have the greatest potential to achieve success?

Off Track

Ask all questions with genuine curiosity.

That is an important point. How does that affect [objective at hand]?

I see the connection. I think we should consider expanding our discussion in that area at another time. Does that sound okay?

Great. You obviously have some good insights, what is the best idea you have heard so far in relation to [objective at hand]?

We sat down to achieve [objective at hand]. So where are we? *or* [Name] please review for us/me what we are trying to accomplish.

Let's write here on the flipchart what we've accomplished so far. [Name], you start.

Accountability

Ask all questions with genuine curiosity.

I'm excited to hear about your progress. Why don't you walk me thorough your action items. Let's start with successes. (You have a copy of what **they** wrote the last time you met.)

It sounds like you've had some challenges. Let's back up for a moment and I'd like to hear about some successes first.

Great job. I'm excited. What did you do differently to achieve these successes?

Okay, now share with me how you did on the rest of the action items.

What did you do first?

How did you get started?

Then what happened?

What does "try harder" mean to you/look like in this situation?

Hindsight is a valuable perspective – it is always easier to see things after the fact. What could you do differently if you could do it over again?

What obstacles got in the way?

[For each obstacle], knowing that can happen, how will you approach it differently?

Is there anything else of which I need to be aware?

Caught Pulling Wool over Supervisor's Eyes

Ask all questions with genuine curiosity.
When you said [   ], what did you mean?
When you see a problem like [   ], what do you do?
What types of problems do you see as within your area of expertise?
How do you feel you could have positively affected the team if you had taken initiative on [   ]?
When you said [   ], what additional information could you have shared with me?
When we speak about a problem or challenge, my expectation is that you will apply your skills, expertise, and ability to address any concerns that are present or that you believe will arise. What expertise did you possess that you could have applied in this situation?
How will you approach similar situations differently in the future?
What other similar situations exist right now in our work environment?

Complete Disagreement

Ask all questions with genuine curiosity.
I get the impression that we really don't agree. I'd really like to hear more. Can you share with me how you see the situation?
Can you share with me where you are coming from?
Have you felt that way for a long time?

What do you think contributes to the problem?

When do you think it started?

How have you been involved?

How would you like to be involved?

What opportunities do you have to positively influence the situation?

It seems like we're coming from completely different angles. What is most important to you?

What do you feel should never change?

What must be different in your opinion?

What do you feel will never change?

I believe we can find common ground. From what you've said, we appear to agree on (A, B, C). Does that sound correct?

Where are the areas that you think we'll just need to agree to disagree?

How will that affect our company performance?

How will that impact your job performance?

Reading inspires thought.
Thought leads to ideas.
Ideas generate action.
Action happens one step at a time.
The first step is the most difficult
to determine and to take.

What are the first steps you will take as a result of reading this article?

1. _____
2. _____
3. _____

When the Conversation is Not over…

Hey! Has anyone ever wrapped up a conversation you were not done having? Have you felt like you were making progress in a discussion only to have the person to whom you were speaking decide the results were good enough and leave?

Results. An effective conversation has great results. However, you cannot stay in a conversation forever, waiting for those great results to happen. People wear out. Some people will talk forever and never arrive at a solution. Others will talk for a minute or two and be done discussing a situation.

Personalities. Depending on which of those descriptions more accurately represents you, you might find yourself either ending a conversation when the person with whom you are speaking is not done, or needing a longer conversation than the other person is willing to tolerate.

If either person in a conversation is not done, that need must be identified and acted upon in order to bring about the desired long term results.

What to do?

It *is okay* to wrap up the conversation when the agreed upon time frame has expired, either person needs to leave, or one person is done.

It is *not okay* to ignore someone's need to continue the conversation at a later time.

It *is a good idea* to take a break if one person needs it, and acknowledge you are doing so in order to ensure productive use of everyone's time.

It *is not a good idea* to leave without some type of summary.

It *is a good idea* to determine next steps for each meeting participant.

First, ensure you start the conversation with a clear goal in mind. That goal can be referenced to keep the conversation on track, identify next steps, and if needed, determine the need, and the agenda, for a follow-up meeting.

Then, when there is either 10% of the meeting time left or when one person becomes restless, start to summarize what has been accomplished, identify any unmet needs and schedule a follow-up meeting if needed at a future date. The steps each person will take before the next meeting, and the agenda for the follow-up meeting should be clearly identified, committed to and agreed upon by everyone involved.

Simply escaping a conversation does not mean it has finished, and could cost you a lot more time in the long run.

Reading inspires thought.
Thought leads to ideas.
Ideas generate action.
Action happens one step at a time.
The first step is the most difficult
to determine and to take.

What are the first steps you will take as a result of reading this article?

1. _____

2. _____

3. _____

Getting out of a Conversation

It seems like there are always plenty of parties, events and gatherings in the business world. And while it is good fun to visit with friends and family, in the business setting the professional who attends many events probably does so with a business agenda in mind. While still enjoyable, the event also turns into an opportunity to build current relationships, initiate new connections and discuss business opportunities.

When you wish to accomplish those objectives, getting 'stuck' in a non-strategic conversation can be a problem. It's important to have a chance to speak with each person at an event who is important to your success.

Why do we get 'stuck'?

- There are a lot of people who are not good at getting *into* conversations, so they don't want to leave the security of the one they are in.
  If this is you...get out there, make eye contact, shake a hand, go get food or drink – and start a new conversation.

- Maybe the person with whom you are speaking does not think you have learned enough about them and their company yet!
  If this is you, this is a major networking mistake. Ask more questions about the other person to build a relationship. Talk less and you will be considered much more interesting.

- The person with whom you are speaking is not there to make multiple connections, just to socialize.
  If this is you, more power to you! Enjoy yourself, and also open the door for the other person to leave if they are looking for more concrete results from their attendance at the event.

- You don't want to hurt their feelings by cutting them off and speaking before they are finished.
  If this is you, realize that many people will speak to fill the silence, and may be relieved if you end the conversation.

How can you politely get out of a conversation?

- *Start with a phrase such as:*
  It was good talking to you…
  I have enjoyed our conversation…
  I was surprised to learn (something you learned about them…)
  I hope your (vacation, business venture, event they mentioned) goes well…

- *And finish the sentence with something that says you are thinking about them.*

I will let you go mingle and meet some more of the attendees.

I would like you to meet... (Identify someone you want to introduce them to and take them there.)

- *Or finish the sentence with something you need to do.*
I'm going to go try that delicious food.
I'm going to go get myself something to drink.
If you'll excuse me, I see someone I need to catch up with.

There is no requirement that you stay in a conversation for as long as it can possibly last. Especially in a business setting, most people have objectives in their head for what they'd like to accomplish.

Have you ever felt 'stuck' in a conversation?

Reading inspires thought.
Thought leads to ideas.
Ideas generate action.
Action happens one step at a time.
The first step is the most difficult
to determine and to take.

What are the first steps you will take as a result of reading this article?

1. _____
2. _____
3. _____

HOW not IF

Motivating your Team Members

Section Overview

The objective of motivating your team members is to enable them to achieve great things, benefiting themselves, the team and the organization. But, you can't actually motivate others. As the leader, you _can_ facilitate the process of helping others uncover their potential. These conversations are often difficult because they push people into areas outside their comfort zone, and possibly beyond what they realize they are capable of achieving. The articles in this section offer insights on deciding 'If' you will act in ways that motivate others, as well as various ways 'How' you can connect with those people important to your success. Any great change happens one step at a time and determination is required. Although determination and persistence are not foreign to any good leader, this process can be slower than an ambitious leader would prefer.

Many people are seen as lazy because they are hitting obstacles they cannot overcome alone. For the benefit of the team, you owe it to employees to kick them in the pants when you think they are lazy. You, or someone else, saw potential when you hired them! Especially in challenging situations, employees crave and require your leadership to make it through.

With the determination to become more effective at motivating your team members, let's explore 'How,' not 'If' to get it done, one step at a time.

The Top Three Myths of Motivating Others

Do You Talk Too Much?

People motivate themselves. However, there are things that leaders can do to facilitate the process.

But first, let's examine a few common myths:

Myth #1: *People are motivated by an energetic, enthusiastic leader.*
Some people are, and some just find that level of energy annoying or downright exhausting. This energetic leader may get others excited about what they are doing, but rarely will this excitement alone result in the person displaying lasting motivation. And, it can be very difficult for a leader to maintain that level of enthusiasm, when they are expected to be the fuel for everyone's fire all the time.

Myth #2: *People are motivated by fear of repercussions.*
People would much rather experience all kinds of terrible repercussions than go through the painful process of changing their behaviors. If it is easy to change their behaviors only enough to avoid being

fired, people may do that, but will never be motivated by their fear to do any more than the minimum required amount of work.

Myth #3: *People are motivated by hearing how important it is to get things done.*
It's true that people are motivated when they are excited about the expected results, ambitious goals and the vision and mission of the organization. However, the motivation does not necessarily appear because they *heard* about the expected results or vision/mission. Very few people will become motivated for longer than a brief time when they only *hear* something. Most people will agree that those who are motivated take action. Motivating others means they are inspired toward action. There is a long distance between hearing something and doing it.

*Therefore, in order motivate others, you need to find a way to get them **to talk** and **to do;** and ensure they experience success, however small, as a result.*

To Talk and To Do:

1. *Stop Talking.* If you want to communicate a message, speak some and then stop. Ask questions and have a conversation which includes getting the other person talking. Get them talking about the importance of the project/task, the possible methods for getting it done, the obstacles they see, the fears they have and the first steps they will take.

2. ***Make First Steps Happen.*** In order to get started, people often need to be 'forced' to take the first step. The fear of the unknown or perfectionist tendencies lead to procrastination. Laziness is often a misnomer. As their manager, you might need to determine the first step together, decide on a deadline and hold them to it. When they experience success, their motivation level will increase.

What successes have you experienced in motivating others? What challenges do you face? Do you talk too much in your efforts to motivate others? Are you effective at holding others accountable?

Reading inspires thought.
Thought leads to ideas.
Ideas generate action.
Action happens one step at a time.
The first step is the most difficult
to determine and to take.

What are the first steps you will take as a result of reading this article?

1. _____
2. _____
3. _____

What Do Elephant Eaters and Leaders Have in Common?

How do you eat an elephant? *One bite at a time, of course.* How do you lead people? *One step at a time.* Whether you are communicating expectations, recognizing good performance, or hoping to change poor behaviors, it is most effectively accomplished in small steps.

You may start an employee's career with a splashy orientation that covers your company's mission, vision, strategic objectives, policies and procedures. However, most employees receive so much information in their first week or two, they find it hard to digest. Long term, as their manager, they need to hear from you, every day in little bites, about how those company objectives apply to them and their every day activities.

Recognition is a great way to inspire employees. When you acknowledge the good things they do, they will try to do these good things more often. End of year awards are fine, but daily recognition of desired behaviors allows you to communicate your expectations in manageable bites. There are a great number of opportunities for recognition: at regular meetings, when a customer expresses satisfaction, with a note on their paycheck, and at special events and celebrations. Overall, whenever you interact with your employees is an opportunity to recognize specific desired behaviors.

Small Bites

If you want to improve employee performance, you want to change their behaviors. No one wants to, or is even capable of, changing overnight. Therefore, after being very sure of what behaviors you want to see, you must communicate these expectations repetitively, in small bites.

As a leader, you routinely face obstacles. It is easy to be overcome by frustration. However, obstacles need to be addressed quite like the above objectives - one bite at a time. Trying to tackle a challenge with all your resources at one time may be effective. But most obstacles require you chip away at them over time.

Being an effective leader requires patience, with a healthy dose of persistence. Realizing most things cannot be accomplished overnight, especially when other people are involved, leads you to the logical approach of addressing challenges one bite at a time - exactly how you'd eat an elephant *(if ever you were faced with such a feat)*.

Reading inspires thought.
Thought leads to ideas.
Ideas generate action.
Action happens one step at a time.
The first step is the most difficult
to determine and to take.

What are the first steps you will take as a result of reading this article?

1. _____

2. _____

3. _____

Energizing your Front Line Employees – Have You Given Up?

Bringing out the best in your employees is not easy, is often disregarded as impossible and is seen as a lower priority than a lot of other tasks on managers' things to do lists.

None of us walk into a job being the best we can be on our first day. None of us learn in a box and without help from others. None of us will continue to be successful if we do not learn and grow. And none of us are so self-inspired that we can achieve our potential without inspiration, insight, wisdom and a good kick in the pants from someone else.

Yet professional development is often seen as something reserved for upper management and skills training as more applicable to the front line employee.

But what about energizing your employees to do their current job better than you or they thought possible?

What energizes people?

Here are a few ideas:
- Work they enjoy

- Working with people they like and trust

- Achieving more and performing better than yesterday

- Learning something new

- Meeting and exceeding expectations set by someone they respect

- Being recognized and rewarded for a job well done

- Finally achieving something with which they were struggling

- Accomplishing a goal they felt was just out of reach

- Mastering a task or skill

What have you done today to energize your employees? Where have you provided them opportunity to learn and grow? Have you created an energizing environment?

Reading inspires thought.
Thought leads to ideas.
Ideas generate action.
Action happens one step at a time.
The first step is the most difficult
to determine and to take.

What are the first steps you will take as a result of reading this article?

1. _____
2. _____
3. _____

You Owe it to Them!

There are many benefits to the employee who focuses on their own professional development including promotion, pay raise, career enhancement, and a feeling of accomplishment.

Managers often talk about professional development because it is the right thing to do. The reality is that it's hard work on the employee, so it is often overlooked.

As a manager, you owe it to your employees to assist them in their professional development:

- Ask about their goals. If they don't know, help them by asking where they'd like to be in ten years, what they enjoy doing the most, or what position they aspire to achieve. Help them dream a little!

- Ask what they'd like to learn more about.

- Ask what steps they are taking or would like to take to learn those things and achieve their goals.

- Ask how you can help.

- Help them set specific, measurable, achievable milestones in their roles at work.

- Follow up and hold them accountable. Yes, that's your job. It's too hard for anyone to do it alone and they may have no one else but you to fill that role.

Your rewards for this effort are happier, more productive, more effective employees who consistently add ever-increasing benefits to your bottom line.

Reading inspires thought.
Thought leads to ideas.
Ideas generate action.
Action happens one step at a time.
The first step is the most difficult
to determine and to take.

What are the first steps you will take as a result of reading this article?

1. _____
2. _____
3. _____

A Strength or a Skill?

The Frustrated Top Performer

Janice is a whiz at taking notes, summarizing what happened in a meeting of 20 people going in all directions, and pinpointing not only the most important points, but the action items upon which everyone agreed. Strategically, she asks key questions throughout the meeting to clarify points, expands conversation to alleviate confusion and isolates what needs to be acted upon.

Because of her brilliant abilities to do this tough task, Janice is often asked to assume this role. The problem is, Janice really does not like to take the notes, is worn out by the process and is bored in that role especially because it prevents her from actively sharing her opinions in the meeting. She is skilled, but taking notes is not her strength.

What is a Strength?

A strength is something that energizes you.

Think about the times you are excited to be at work, times you really feel full of energy for what you are doing and despite difficulties, you can keep working at a task that is truly challenging. Those are the times you are working with your strengths.

You may not be exceptionally talented in your areas of strength, but the fact is that you are energized by doing the task, by working to improve, and possess a great deal of resilience to continue to push forward.

What is a Skill?
On the other hand, a skill is something that you are good at doing. Maybe through innate ability, or a lot of practice or hard work, you have built this skill. And it certainly feels good to be successful at something. But, the activity is not necessarily exciting for you and you don't look forward to it.

Each individual needs to identify their strengths and pinpoint their skills. Then, the greatest part about a strength is that you are eager to work very hard to improve your performance because you enjoy the process. *And* you have enormous potential to significantly improve your performance in an area of strength. Seize that opportunity and ensure your employees do the same!

Reading inspires thought.
Thought leads to ideas.
Ideas generate action.
Action happens one step at a time.
The first step is the most difficult
to determine and to take.

What are the first steps you will take as a result of reading this article?

1. _____

2. _____

3. _____

Identifying Strengths & Skills

Skills are activities you are good at doing, but do not necessarily enjoy. Strengths energize you, but you may not be extremely good at them. *However, strengths are where you have the greatest opportunity to improve your performance because they energize you.*

The question is: How do you know which is which?

Observe carefully.
If you take a moment to observe your team as they go about their daily duties, you will see the times when their faces light up, when they begin to work a bit quicker and when they put their nose to the grindstone and stay focused and determined. Those are the times they are working within their areas of strength.

Listen carefully.
Listen to how your team members speak about certain tasks and roles. Are they animated, thoughtful and asking good questions? When do they talk more than usual? When do they think more than usual? These are times where they are probably talking about their strengths.

Start a discussion.

After you've observed and listened to those with whom you work, ask them what they enjoy doing the most. If you ask them to do a task or assist you in a certain project area, notice how they approach it and then ask them afterwards if they enjoyed what they did. If they respond with, "Sure, no problem," ask more questions to clarify. "I really appreciate your assistance and need your expertise, but it seems like you'd rather I was able to do it on my own or have someone else help me?" Then, be ready to do so.

People on Your Team

People-pleasers. The challenge with the above activities is that there are personality types that make pinpointing strengths difficult. There are people who will never say "No!" would never admit they did not want to help and will always step in with a smile. You must observe them much more carefully in order to see what is truly energizing to them, and what they do out of a need to please others. Rarely is the desire to please others their actual strength.

Grouches. The other challenge is those people who have tried very hard to cover any energy they might possess in a veil of grouchiness. In order to protect their ego, their personal space or their fears, they almost always respond with a lack of energy. You may need to watch them carefully for a longer period of time, offer extra recognition and appreciation for what they do well, and encourage the things they are good at to see if you can uncover some energizing activities.

Strengths are not always the things you are best at, but certainly can be. Pinpointing what you are good at can be a decent place to start if you are struggling to identify strengths.

What about you? You can also observe how *you* do and say the things you do and say. Have discussions with your supervisor or peers about what energizes you to identify *your* strengths. What activity are you doing when your energy levels the highest during the day?

Reading inspires thought.
Thought leads to ideas.
Ideas generate action.
Action happens one step at a time.
The first step is the most difficult
to determine and to take.

What are the first steps you will take as a result of reading this article?

1. _____
2. _____
3. _____

Do You Have Lazy Employees?

Managers often complain that employees are inherently lazy. I think we all relish our downtime and floating in the pool, putting your feet in the sand or curling up on the couch is good for all of us. But, in a work situation, I most often see people called lazy who I believe to instead be nervous, scared of failure and in general, hiding in their comfort zone.

Comfort Zone

Each person's comfort zone is a mentally comfortable place where certain known and secure behaviors produce steady performance and an absence of a sense of risk within certain acceptable boundaries. This sense of comfort comes from predictability and known consequences which create the low risk, low stress environment.

Frank is seen by his supervisor as lazy because he will not take on any duties outside his specific job description. He may even tell coworkers and himself that he is "lazy" and that's why he doesn't do more, doesn't strive for those awards or company goals and really isn't too worried about receiving an average evaluation. Without turning into a psychologist, if we had the crystal ball into his history, we might see that in the past Frank had stepped up and tried new things, experimented with crazy ideas and 'jumped right in' to offer suggestions. He got burned, was yelled at for messing things up, failed once, and discovered how much hard work it is to learn something new.

Whatever his history and his reasons, Frank is comfortable doing what he is doing, content with calling himself "lazy" to keep others from pushing him to do more, and secure with his current mediocre performance because he avoids failure.

Managers and leaders have the potential to bring out the greatness in others!
Think of the laziest employee you have:

- What skills are they missing?

- What are they afraid to try? Why are they afraid to try?

- How do you react if they mess up? Is it okay to fail and try again?

- What have you done to encourage and insist upon their professional development and continuous improvement, no matter how small the steps?

Are they lazy or just hiding in their comfort zone?

Reading inspires thought.
Thought leads to ideas.
Ideas generate action.
Action happens one step at a time.
The first step is the most difficult
to determine and to take.

What are the first steps you will take as a result of reading this article?

1. _____

2. _____

3. _____

Laziness is often a Misnomer

Managers use laziness as a reason why employees don't do a good job or complete tasks they are assigned. Maybe you have uttered the accusation, "(S)he's just lazy!" Some believe that people in general are lazy.

I couldn't disagree more! People are passionate, driven and intelligent beings! We even see those with great physical and mental limitations accomplish great things, like the world-renown pianist who has a total of only four fingers!

That drive to contribute, accomplish and succeed is in every person. It may be buried deeply behind a lifetime of bad experiences, of hearing words that beat up the self-confidence and a barrage of media messages that promulgate mediocrity.

Any employee who works for you has worked other places before, has interacted with friends and family, and has received messages about what they can accomplish and what is acceptable and expected – for years.

Laziness is defined as averse or disinclined to work, activity, or exertion and slow-moving and sluggish. Why would someone act this way?

1. Failing to do the work in a previous job did not bring any negative results and they continued to receive their paycheck. They watched others work hard and be paid the same thing or be given more work to do.

2. They've worked hard in the past to reach a particular goal and failed, received harsh criticism for doing so, and were not given any coaching or a second chance.

3. They have grown up in a generation who believes they are entitled to a great life and it's easy to get there. Just watch TV and pay attention to the messages, and it's no surprise.

4. They have never found their passion, nor felt really excited about the mission or goals of a company and have never had a leader that connected with them enough to ignite this excitement.

5. No one has ever "forced" them to be successful, by pushing them out of their comfort zone and providing a safety net to assist in their success.

6. They have never worked with a boss who took the time to get to know them, what is important to them and where they are coming from – in order to help them feel part of the team and work to their strengths.

I'm sure there are many reasons why someone would appear 'lazy', and these are just a few. Below are suggestions of how you, as the manager, might address an employee who acts lazy for these reasons.

1. *No negative results in the past.* Ensure you are clearly setting expectations, explaining consequences and holding them accountable. Take the time to provide the routine accountability, insist they report on their successes and failures and require they give you an idea of what they can do differently to continue to improve.

2. *Past failures.* Celebrate success and hard work. Even little bits of success and small steps in the right direction should be acknowledged by you. And little failures and small steps in the wrong direction should receive coaching and redirection.

3. *Entitlement.* Realize that your employees may have a different mindset than you, and may not have grown up in a strong environment to teach them otherwise. Do you as the manager need to act like a parent? In the role of imparting values, yes, sometimes you do.

4. *Lack of Passion.* Share the mission and goals, get them talking about them (notice I did not say that you should talk about them), and require they come up with good ideas. Show them through leading by example what passion looks like. All members of your management team need to do so, not only you.

5. *Force Success.* No matter how small, require they do tasks and activities outside their comfort zone, check in with them before they have a chance to fail to redirect them if necessary, and help them to taste success! Your involvement will become less as time goes on.

6. **Bad boss.** The best bosses expect great things, demand excellence, impart passion and excitement and most importantly, connect with their people. They realize that the best processes and systems in the world will have limitations if the employees are not engaged. Engagement requires taking the time to build a relationship. A relationship is a two way street. You must also insist the employee do their part!

Have you had an experience where you thought an employee was lazy, but were able to uncover a motivated person by using techniques like those listed above?

Reading inspires thought.
Thought leads to ideas.
Ideas generate action.
Action happens one step at a time.
The first step is the most difficult
to determine and to take.

What are the first steps you will take as a result of reading this article?

1. _____
2. _____
3. _____

HOW not *IF*

Setting and Communicating Expectations
Section Overview

A key component to working well with others is to know specifically what you want them to do, and be able to communicate that message. The distance from your head to your mouth might not seem like a long way, but so much information is lost during that trip! The fact is, you probably know quite well what you expect, but what is spoken, heard and acted upon might be quite different. We think in pictures and comments, not written instructions.

This series of articles offers insights on clarifying and communicating what you expect in a way that employees can understand, respond to, and be successful in implementing. The most difficult part of these conversations is remembering to have them, and then phrasing things in a way that ensures your message can be received. Decide to make this a priority. It is most likely not a question of 'If' you are doing it well right now. As long as things are not going perfectly, there is almost always a place where expectations have not been communicated fully and it is up to you, the leader, to determine 'How' to communicate what you expect more effectively.

With the determination to become more effective at setting and communicating expectations, let's explore 'How,' not 'If' to get it done, one step at a time.

Leadership by Example

Leading by example is a powerful method of influencing others' behavior in order to improve performance, productivity, effectiveness, efficiency and customer service. How to lead by example in order to be effective starts long before the leader acts at all.

- First, the leader must personally be clear about the company vision, philosophy, objectives and expectations.

- Then, the leader must believe deeply in those items, so they will be genuine in their actions.

- Thirdly, the leader determines what behaviors they must display in order to see complementary behaviors from others.

- Since not only actions are important, the leader must ensure their words match their actions in order to be believed and thought credible.

- The leader must demonstrate these behaviors consistently with employees, peers and customers, over a significant period of time, in order to convince others they are genuine.

- Finally, the leader must recognize appropriate behaviors when they are exhibited by others, in order to confirm their interpretation of the leader's expectations.

Leadership by example is a challenging concept to routinely put into practice, but the effects are incredible! Working through each of these steps can prove extremely helpful to making this type of behavior routine.

Reading inspires thought.
Thought leads to ideas.
Ideas generate action.
Action happens one step at a time.
The first step is the most difficult
to determine and to take.

What are the first steps you will take as a result of reading this article?

1. _____
2. _____
3. _____

The Power of the Leader

"Nearly all men can stand adversity, but if you want to test a person's character, give them power."

- Abraham Lincoln

What do you do with the power you hold as a leader?

You may have the power to hire, fire, and decide compensation and benefits. You may also be able to yell, demand, discipline and suspend. You certainly have the power as the leader to push people around.

You also possess the power to bring out the best in people and help them unleash their potential!

Do you as their leader:

- Set high expectations of your team members?

- Believe they can accomplish more than they believe about themselves?

- Insist they set ambitious individual goals for themselves at work?

- Celebrate success as they make progress and achieve even small milestones?

- Encourage them to continue to improve professionally and support them financially to do so?

- Give them your time and attention to work through problems, to think big and to be innovative?

What you do and what you say has tremendous power to influence those who work for you. Regardless of how much or how little they appear to respect, admire or follow you, you still wield power as their leader and as the person in charge. You might believe that much of the current workforce lacks sincere loyalty to their leader or employer, since they often change jobs and seem not to care much about the view of those in charge. That might lead you to believe that you don't have much power as a leader. That is not necessarily the case. You would be mistaken if you missed your opportunity to use the power you have as a leader to motivate, inspire, and believe in your team.

I believe that 95% of workers never reach their potential. What are you doing as their leader to help them to see the possibilities and reach for those ambitious dreams?

Reading inspires thought.
Thought leads to ideas.
Ideas generate action.
Action happens one step at a time.
The first step is the most difficult
to determine and to take.

What are the first steps you will take as a result of reading this article?

1. _____
2. _____
3. _____

Ready....Action!

When your employees do not do what you want them to, ask yourself the question: "Do they really know and understand what I want?" Then think very carefully before you answer.

Sure, the employees know you don't want them to be late because that's what you have told them. However, their understanding of what that means may be different than yours:

"I am not late. My tires hit the parking lot at 8:00am. It's not my fault I'm not sitting at my desk working until 8:20am. I would have had to run over a coworker to arrive here any quicker!"
or
"I'm at my desk at 8:00am, but then I just need to make a couple quick phone calls and catch up with others in the office. What's the big deal? It builds the team, doesn't it?"
or
"Yes, I know my boss doesn't want me to be late, but if I'm 20 -30 minutes late, nobody really seems to mind,

so they must mean *more than 30 minutes* late is truly late."

This scenario leaves many opportunities for the manager to make their expectations more clear.

1. People in general find it hard **not** to do something. Explain what it is you *want* them to do in terms of the behavior you want to see.

2. Secondly, employees' definition of late may differ from yours as their manager. You believe that on time means that you are sitting at your desk at 8:00am, working.

3. If you do not see what you expect, then you *must* follow up and clarify your expectations. If the behavior goes uncorrected, the employee will assume they are meeting your expectations.

The example above is a simple one, and the concepts can be applied to every expectation you'd like to communicate. A great place to start thinking about expectations is with the times your employees do something of which you do not approve. Ask yourself what you would have preferred they did instead. This forces you to picture and describe what the right behavior looks like in action, which is a crucial step to defining your expectations.

Reading inspires thought.
Thought leads to ideas.
Ideas generate action.
Action happens one step at a time.
The first step is the most difficult
to determine and to take.

What are the first steps you will take as a result of reading this article?

1. _____
2. _____
3. _____

What do you want?

Translation is the ability to take what's in your head and communicate it effectively to the people who you want to do it. Managers often struggle with getting their employees to do what they want. When they try to delve into what they specifically want the employee to do, they have a hard time describing it in detail. This is not unusual! But, it is a stumbling block to success; an impenetrable wall, in fact.

You have a vision of how you would like things to happen.

Often the 'How to get it done' is very fuzzy because when you personally get it done, you just make it happen.

The bad news: There is no way around specific instruction and delegation. Yes, with the more capable employees, they are able to take initiative based on minimal instruction, but that minimal instruction must still be clear. If you wait for the perfect employees to be able to take your vision and implement it, it will definitely delay your growth plans. Growth requires both vision and ability to implement. If you want someone to implement your vision instead of their own, you need to be able to explain it to them in a way they clearly understand. Because you see it so clearly, this may seem monotonous.

The Quandary: Deal with some monotony, but have endless opportunity; or deal only with your brilliant vision and do it yourself.

Reading inspires thought.
Thought leads to ideas.
Ideas generate action.
Action happens one step at a time.
The first step is the most difficult
to determine and to take.

What are the first steps you will take as a result of reading this article?

1. _____

2. _____

3. _____

What Do You Want Me to Do?

If you never tell your employees what you expect, you'll never get what you expect. Even when you tell them what you expect, you may not get it!

Communicating expectations is crucial to being a successful manager. Ask yourself what you really expect from the employee. Then, tell them what that is. That may sound very basic, but it is often overlooked.

Start at the beginning. The interview is not only a chance for you to discover the fit between the potential hire and the position to be filled, it is also a great time to explore their expectations about the job and communicate what you expect.

For example, Mark accepted the job of a housekeeper at a local hotel. He fully expected to clean rooms and replenish supplies. In the interview, Mark's supervisor Larry had asked him questions about his experience with cleaning rooms and his familiarity with various cleaning agents. They also spoke about the schedule and wages. It was never explained to Mark that he could play a crucial role in guest relations and problem solving, promoting the in-hotel restaurant and explaining ancillary hotel services, where extra revenue was generated.

Over time, Larry became frustrated with Mark's lack of 'initiative'. Finally, at evaluation time, Larry communicated his disappointment with Mark's performance. Mark was shocked. He was hired to clean rooms and replenish supplies and he was doing that just fine. Larry realized the miscommunication and began to explain to Mark the other roles he could play as he went about his daily routine.

As a result of this conversation, Mark began to notice unhappy clients to whom he could offer help or make suggestions. He began to see these things as part of his job.

As the manager, ask yourself what you *really expect* from your employees. Think through the tasks and the roles that you expect the employee to fulfill. Then, tell them what these are!

Reading inspires thought.
Thought leads to ideas.
Ideas generate action.
Action happens one step at a time.
The first step is the most difficult
to determine and to take.

What are the first steps you will take as a result of reading this article?

1. _____
2. _____
3. _____

What Not To Do

Are there things that you would like your employees to stop doing? Do you tell them to stop doing those things? Do they hear you? Do they change their behavior?

It is critically important to pinpoint specific *behaviors* that you wish would stop. "You better change your bad attitude!" is a personal attack *and* not specific enough. Instead, "When you are in the staff meeting, I see you roll your eyes, exude an audible sigh and cross your arms in response to an idea you do not like. This is not an acceptable response from any member of the team." The employee must be confronted about behaviors you see as unacceptable.

However, it cannot stop there. As critical as it is to pinpoint what the unacceptable behavior specifically looks like, you must also do more than that!

You must tell them what you want them to do instead.

Can't they figure that out on their own?
Maybe, but if they knew what to do or how to act more professionally, they might be doing it already. "Really,

156

boss, when Sam brings up such an outrageous idea, I just react that way naturally. What do you expect me to do when he is saying dumb stuff?"

They know what to do. They are just being difficult and not doing it.
If this is the case, then when you give them specific behaviors you wish to see instead, you can hold them accountable to these firm expected behaviors. Otherwise, they may stop doing annoying behavior #1 (eye rolls, sigh, crossed arms), which you asked them to stop, and start doing annoying behavior #2 (laugh and start texting).

I don't have the time to explain every little thing they need to do!
Then teach them to think. Ask them a question or two, get them thinking and next time, you can expect them to think a bit more about what they are doing. "How do you think it affects the rest of the team when you roll your eyes, sigh and cross your arms?" "What could you do to control your reaction and your outward appearance?"

After they speak, you can make a specific suggestion: "If you think an idea is not credible, take a second to think before you respond, stop and take note of what you are doing with your eyes, voice and arms. Keep your arms open and on the table, your voice silent and your eyes on your notepad. It may also help to jot down in your notes why you think the idea is crazy and address those situations with me (your supervisor) outside our staff meeting or with the individual themselves."

There are times when a small situation may simply require that you communicate to the employee that a specific behavior was unacceptable and they should not do it again. But chances are that there are more chronic behaviors employees exhibit that you do not like, and those will never be corrected without a conversation about what they are to do instead.

What do your employees do that you wish they would stop? Do they know what to do instead? Have you held them accountable to specific alternate behaviors?

Reading inspires thought.
Thought leads to ideas.
Ideas generate action.
Action happens one step at a time.
The first step is the most difficult
to determine and to take.

What are the first steps you will take as a result of reading this article?

1. _____
2. _____
3. _____

Deadlines!!

Most likely you are very effective at personally meeting deadlines, even if it requires juggling priorities, working long hours and multitasking. Why is it that your employees are not as good at meeting the deadlines that you expect them to meet? Why don't they get things done when you expect?

If you face this challenge, you are not alone. Managers at all levels of success, lengths of time as a leader, and experience levels, suffer with this same difficulty.

Think about the process. When you ask an employee to do something:

- the message comes from your brain and must travel to your mouth
- along the way it is affected by what's distracting you and your ability to explain.
- The employee hears your words and
- sees your body language and nonverbal signals (including subtle ones which you may not even realize exist),

- receives the message through the filter of what else is on their mind,

- understands what you say given their experience and frame of reference

- and registers the message in their brain.

This is a long and complicated journey.

What may be lost is exactly **when** you want this done. You may have an idea in your head of a date or time, but you may not mention it, assuming the employee knows it's important and that they know what 'important' means to you in terms of delivery date.

Ask Yourself:

- Have I told them specifically what task I want them to complete, especially if it is outside their normal responsibility?

- Have I given them a specific deadline?

- Have I left any ambiguity?

This does not mean that we fail to allow our employees to make intelligent decisions or have some freedom in how they operate. It does however, mean that if they are not doing what we expect, when we expect it, we must first go back and audit our own style of delivering the message in the first place.

This week, try giving a specific date as a deadline for a draft, for a finished product, for the first step in the process, or for the next step in the process. People most often arrange their priorities based on what appears urgent, which most often is the task with a solid deadline to which they will be held accountable.

Then, ask a few questions to see if they have understood the expectation. When you delegate or set an expectation, you could ask the employee to just repeat it back to you, but that is demeaning and doesn't necessarily mean they really understand it.

Test Understanding

Instead, ask open ended questions in a curious and nurturing way to get them talking so you can hear what they are thinking. *Ask all questions with genuine curiosity.*

What do you think is the best way to approach this?
What is the first piece you are going to tackle? What is the first step you will take?
What is your biggest concern about that?
When would you expect to have that part completed?
It needs to be done in 30 days; can you map out how you plan to schedule the work?
What do you need from me?
What is it that I can do to help/support you?
Why don't you email me with your status update by noon on Friday?
Stop into my office right after lunch on Tuesday and give me a progress report.
What do you expect to be the hardest part?
What is one question that you have?
What will you need to do differently than what you have been doing?

How will you approach this differently than the last project like this?

How do you feel we can do this even better/more successfully?

By asking even just a few of these questions, you may either be pleasantly surprised with the plan in their head or shocked at how little they really understood the urgency, important milestones and timeline.

Reading inspires thought.
Thought leads to ideas.
Ideas generate action.
Action happens one step at a time.
The first step is the most difficult
to determine and to take.

What are the first steps you will take as a result of reading this article?

1. _____
2. _____
3. _____

HOW not IF

Managing your Team
Section Overview

Successful leadership starts with a strong vision and values, both on a company and department level. Inspiring employees to buy into the vision and values creates a more passionate team. In this section the importance of that vision is explored, as well as how to effectively channel the resulting strong determination of individuals. Combining individual's strengths, ideas, expertise and approaches to achieve a common purpose is one of the most challenging parts of pulling a team together. It is also a big opportunity for productive conflict that creates the best solutions. Insights on avoiding the turf wars and building the team are offered in this section.

Situations of conflict such as these inevitably lead to difficult conversations. Navigating through these conversations yields significant rewards as the expertise and passion of each person is combined to achieve great things. Don't be that professional who shies away from these conversations and decides 'If' you will participate. Seek out opportunities and learn 'How' to find innovative ideas and strategies within these situations.

The uniqueness of each individual can present both opportunity and challenges for managers to interact well with other managers and coworkers. Every workplace is diverse and the best managers develop people to be able to play nicely in the sandbox.

With the determination to become more effective at managing your team,
let's explore 'How,' not 'If' to get it done, one step at a time.

Decision Making Is Easy

Years ago, during an orientation at a nursing facility, the owner stressed how the residents in our facility always came first in all that we did and the decisions we made. He stressed how it was easiest for all departments to work together, even when they came from very different perspectives, if they focused on making decisions that resulted in what was best for the resident.

This approach is enormously powerful. When managers speak about decisions with which they are struggling, the conversation must continually come back to the vision, purpose and focus of the company. Essentially, many people do not clearly understand this vision, purpose and focus and therefore struggle with decisions.

In order to consider a decision a good one, it must be in line with the vision, purpose and focus of the company. If not, it was a bad decision.

The vision, purpose and focus are not debatable and do not change over time. However, the implementation of that vision does evolve. As the business grows, the way the vision is realized and put into action evolves with new opportunities that arise.

A strong vision is one that guides all company actions, budgets and processes. If a new opportunity, although potentially lucrative, does not fit the focus and the vision of the company, it should not be pursued.

This applies to leaders and managers throughout the company. Each department leader needs to develop and formalize *their* vision for *their* team, which aligns with a larger company vision, purpose and focus. Leaders have a challenging job to do and many rarely make the time to assure the clarity of their vision, purpose and focus. However, decision making would become much easier with a crystal clear vision, about which they are passionate.

Reading inspires thought.
Thought leads to ideas.
Ideas generate action.
Action happens one step at a time.
The first step is the most difficult
to determine and to take.

What are the first steps you will take as a result of reading this article?

1. _____
2. _____
3. _____

If Change is Difficult, You are Doing a Great Job!

Change should be difficult. If not, it means employees are not invested in what you are currently doing, or knew a long time ago you needed to change the way things were done and it took you entirely too long to figure it out.

The most committed employees know why they are doing things a certain way, are committed to the importance of doing it right, and appreciate the need to put forward the effort to consistently perform. Therefore, when you ask them to change, even in order to improve, their investment in doing it the current 'right' way prevents them from adopting change easily. That's a good thing!

A whole different level of thinking is required to comprehend the need to improve, especially before things get really bad. Do you think you have only one angry customer? Many, many unhappy customers never complain. The challenge lies in the fact that you, as the leader destined for success see the need for continuous and preemptive improvement. Failure to realize that 99% of employees will never adopt this belief *to the extent that you will*, will leave you constantly frustrated.

If continuous improvement is one of the fundamentals of how you do business, make sure you are communicating that to employees all the time. Take an inventory. How often is it part of your conversation, your processes, your leadership style and your evaluation of team members? Do you encourage risk-taking on the part of employees for the sake of improvement? How do you react if they fail?

To successfully implement change, realize good employees are invested in the current process, support them as you unfreeze the current behaviors, educate them on the benefits of the change, and then support them as they implement the new methods.

When change is easy you're either *really* fortunate to have an amazing team or you are missing something significant.

Reading inspires thought.
Thought leads to ideas.
Ideas generate action.
Action happens one step at a time.
The first step is the most difficult
to determine and to take.

What are the first steps you will take as a result of reading this article?

1. _____
2. _____
3. _____

Turning Fights into Productive Conversation

When your team members are passionate and excited about accomplishing their goals and making your vision a reality, that's a good thing! That's also when arguments and 'fights' can break out precisely because people are all fired up.

The last thing you want to do is try to subdue that passion and excitement! The fact is that many people are not incredibly effective at communicating. And any skills they did possess have been put aside because they have the need to communicate how strongly they feel about a particular subject.

First, as a group your team needs to acknowledge that these fights happen, even more frequently with some personalities. The supervisors and managers need to agree that the passion is good, and with better communication, both the superior ideas and the cross-department conversation can happen.

Then, the managers need to make sure their team members have appropriate avenues by which to express their great ideas, concerns, suggestions and frustrations. These avenues need to create an environment where it is safe to voice any crazy idea without judgment to ensure the very best ideas are shared. Problems are welcomed and explored because if a passionate team member sees an issue, even if it's not an issue to others, it's important and it will be addressed.

What to do?

Intervention
The manager might pull two people aside who are having a heated conversation and offer some support or structure to the conversation to come to a productive conclusion. The fact is that there is a lot of great information in a conversation like this and sometimes it takes a third person to hear the points each person is presenting. The third person outlines what has been shared to help each person see the other's points. The manager leads the discussion about how the points interrelate and together they find the best solution; better than either could have come up with on their own.

A Designated Time
The manager might also provide time in a weekly staff meeting or daily huddle (depending on the frequency of these heated conversations) for discussion of ideas, suggestions or problems to be solved. The whole team knows this is the place for these conversations, and that they are expected to bring ideas and contribute. They also agree to play by the rules.

Set the Rules

Each person may agree to:

Avoid personal attacks by holding conversations about what someone did, not who they are.

- Voice concerns about an idea and not translate these into concerns about the person's capabilities, motivations or knowledge.

- Wait a certain length of time for each person to make their point.

- Paraphrase what the person who has spoken has said before the next person begins.

- Table some topics until further information can be gathered.

- Be willing to do some 'homework' or research on the issue before the next conversation.

If you have a good team, passions rise and tempers may flare. Acknowledge that, give it a place to happen and set the rules to ensure productive conversation and great solutions result.

Are you able to facilitate productive conversation among your passionate employees?

Reading inspires thought.
Thought leads to ideas.
Ideas generate action.
Action happens one step at a time.
The first step is the most difficult
to determine and to take.

What are the first steps you will take as a result of reading this article?

1. _____
2. _____
3. _____

A Little Fighting is Okay?

There are natural tensions between employees in a company for good reason. There are experts in each department within an organization focused on specific objectives they are expected to achieve, which differ from other departments' goals.

Consider a car. The brakes on a car must effectively stop the vehicle. Otherwise the car will crash. When I step on the gas, I want the car to go. I expect that system to run well. There are times when I need to slam on the brakes and other times when I need to accelerate rapidly.

However, in order for a car to be a pleasure to drive, each one of its components must function well, at the appropriate time in order for me to travel from point A to point B and enjoy the ride.

The problem occurs when department members are so focused on their own particular department objectives that they fail to work together toward company goals. No matter how much I value the contribution of both the brakes and the accelerator,

I cannot use them both at the same time and not worry about the consequences.

As the leader, it is up to you to set the expectations about interdepartmental behavior. You need to lead by example and even teach others how to interact effectively.

Focus on the company's larger goals.
If the goal is to increase the widgets produced per month, then each department needs to focus on their contribution to that goal and how that contribution can be strengthened by the efforts of others.

Address the Elephant in the Room.
If you have tensions between two departments that are obvious to everyone, meet with the leaders of those departments together, ensure a commitment to fix the problem regardless of how often it happens elsewhere, and put a plan together to begin mending fences.

    a. ***Fun events.*** Create an environment that encourages employees to talk with one another and see each other as individuals.

    b. ***Planned communication.*** Set interdepartmental workgroups to ensure the meeting of the brilliant minds takes place and work does not happen based on assumptions or best guesses.

    c. ***Address individual unacceptable behaviors.*** Managers must be prepared to assist employees who are causing trouble to understand the consequences of their actions, help them to be more effective in their approach, and hold them accountable for implementing those changes in behavior.

d. ***Teach what you think is obvious.*** Communication is a skill that everyone assumes they understand and do well, and yet it is at the root of many company issues, the heart of many obstacles and the basis for much tension. Provide educational opportunities to improve their listening and conflict resolution skills.

What does 'fighting' look like in your organization?

Reading inspires thought.
Thought leads to ideas.
Ideas generate action.
Action happens one step at a time.
The first step is the most difficult
to determine and to take.

What are the first steps you will take as a result of reading this article?

1. _____
2. _____
3. _____

A Story about Everybody, Somebody, Anybody, and Nobody

This is a little story about four people named Everybody, Somebody, Anybody, and Nobody.

There was an important job to be done and Everybody was asked to do it.

Everybody was sure that Somebody would do it.

Anybody could have done it, but Nobody did it.

When Nobody did it, Somebody got angry because it was Everybody's job.

Everybody thought Anybody could do it, but Nobody realized that Somebody wouldn't do it.

It ended up that Everybody blamed Somebody when Nobody did what Anybody could have done.

Does this ring any bells in your company? Are your expectations, responsibilities and processes clearly defined?

In your Company...

- What is it that Nobody does or Nobody does well? Why is that?

- What is it that Anybody can do? Are these more simple tasks ignored?

- What is it that Everybody should be doing? How consistently are those mission-critical 'ways of doing business' being followed?

- Who is the Somebody who does Everybody's job? Why do they do that?

- Who is the Somebody who doesn't do their job? Are you accepting that instead of holding them accountable?

- Which job can Nobody do well? Why is it so challenging?

Out of this funny little story come some thought-provoking questions about what gets done and what does not get done, and by whom, in our organizations. How does your organization handle these challenges?

Reading inspires thought.
Thought leads to ideas.
Ideas generate action.
Action happens one step at a time.
The first step is the most difficult
to determine and to take.

What are the first steps you will take as a result of reading this article?

1. _____

2. _____

3. _____

Do Your Managers Handle Diversity Well?

When I search the internet for 'workplace diversity', results include avoiding discrimination on the basis of race, gender, age, and religion. Multicultural workplaces and the global marketplace are also popular discussion topics.

Tip of the Iceberg
Should managers treat people differently because of their race, gender, age, religion or country of origin? I say, "Of course!" People are *all unique* and should all be interacted with as individuals. The qualifiers that have been pulled out in the legal world are only the *tip of that iceberg.*

The Challenge of Leading a Team of Individuals
Managers have the challenge of dealing with a group of individuals. If they all look alike, that only serves to provide a false sense of security and comfort for the manager. That group can be just as challenging to manage since they are all individuals with their own experiences, beliefs, and histories.

Leadership is about interacting effectively with members of the team to accomplish business results. Plain and simple, leadership is about people, people are all different from one another, and similarities often only delude you into thinking you are effectively communicating with another person.

A leader's success level results from their ability to genuinely connect with all the individuals on their team to the extent that they enable that person to access their potential to become the best employee they can be, while keeping them focused on their role in achieving the business goals.

Connect Well
In order to connect well, a manager must:

1. Listen to the employee with genuine interest and be acutely aware of any assumptions they are making about an individual, both positive and negative.

2. Engage the employee in conversation to learn where the employee is coming from in order to lead them in a productive direction.

3. Encourage creativity and innovative solutions while diligently pursuing a strong and clear set of goals, within a defined way of doing business (values and culture).

4. Provide a structure of accountability that is fair but demanding, enforcing this company culture through a series of productive conver-

sations to address employees' concerns and varying approaches.

5. Take this aggressive and discerning communication approach to each and every employee to avoid the legal headaches, but also because it is the right thing to do *if you want to bring out the best in each and every employee!*

Many hard-charging, driven managers who experience a great deal of success will eventually hit a wall because of challenges with their effectiveness in motivating their team to higher levels of productivity and effectiveness. Upper management often has been trained, mentored or self taught to be more effective, where middle managers may be limited unless their ability to listen, communicate and hold people accountable results in concrete business results.

What does your management team look like? Do they have the skills they need to take the team members in your company to the next level of performance and motivation? Are your managers able to embrace the diversity inherent in every team, whether or not they look alike?

Reading inspires thought.
Thought leads to ideas.
Ideas generate action.
Action happens one step at a time.
The first step is the most difficult
to determine and to take.

What are the first steps you will take as a result of reading this article?

1. _____
2. _____
3. _____

Playing Nice in the Sandbox

Prominent leaders have been known to claim that they can teach many skills to their employees, but cannot teach them how to play nice in the sandbox.

Oh, but you can! The mindset above is a common way of thinking for managers and leaders. As a valedictorian in high school and college who thought the world revolved around book knowledge, I am living proof that you can learn 'to play nice'. Needless to say, you would not have described me as one who knew how to 'play well in the sandbox' when I entered the workforce. Without the mentoring of several important figures in my life, I would have continued to reach a certain level of success because of my competence, but would have been limited in bringing out the very best in myself and in others.

The fact is that playing well in the sandbox requires a set of skills just like any other job task. However, they tend to be a set of skills that managers and leaders do not themselves often possess, so they find it very difficult to teach others. Those who are promoted to a management role because of their stellar performance rarely receive training on communication and conflict resolution!

Here are just a few of the skills that are essential to 'play nice in the sandbox' that are not inherent in everyone's personality, but can be taught:

- *Building self awareness* - Most individuals do not have a high degree of awareness of why they act and react the way they do, especially to the point where they can change their reaction as necessary.

- *Identifying common goals* - Focusing more on daily tasks, many people do not take the time to identify goals, pinpoint what goals are universal to their team or organization, and identify each person's contribution.

- *Earning trust* - There are a variety of ways people describe trustworthy behaviors. One of the most common is that people 'do what they say they will do.' However, in a group of 10 people, ask them for a definition of 'trust', and you will hear a variety of responses. In order to build trust with an individual, you must live up to their definition of trust.

- *Communicating effectively* - Talking to one another is something that seems like it should be really simple. In reality, communication skills such as listening are on the forefront of what people need to learn more about how to do well.

- *Engaging in productive conflict* - Rarely do people say they enjoy conflict. Yet so much productive conversation, innovative thinking and utilization of creative and unique approaches are never seized without a productive discussion that may stem from, or be full of, conflict.

- *Interacting with those very different from you* - Not only do many individuals not have a firm grasp on their own style and how they come across, but seeing the strengths and benefits of others' approaches is challenging to do without some good tools in your tool belt.

- *Increasing confidence by improving one's own performance* - There is only so much that you can improve without continually asking and challenging yourself with what you will learn and do differently. Consistently doing a great job may feel like enough to you. Your life is busy and stressful, and your performance is considered sufficient by your supervisor who may not wish to challenge you or rock the boat if you are doing a good job already. However, without incremental and continuous success and improvements, the confidence of any member of the team can erode, which may result in increased defensiveness.

What other skills have you learned that make you a better sandbox member than you were years ago? What skills have you taught your team that make them easier to work with - resulting in greater success?

Reading inspires thought.
Thought leads to ideas.
Ideas generate action.
Action happens one step at a time.
The first step is the most difficult
to determine and to take.

What are the first steps you will take as a result of reading this article?

1. _____
2. _____
3. _____

HOW <u>not</u> *IF*

Accountability & Delivering Feedback
Section Overview

Feedback is so much more than yearly performance evaluations. However, feedback conversations are some of the most difficult conversations and the most often avoided. But, in order to improve performance, it must be measured, and unacceptable behaviors must be addressed with specific feedback and on a consistent basis. If you find yourself assuming employees' responsibilities, it might be easier to do it yourself in the short run. In the long run, the better answer is to delegate and consistently have the sometimes difficult accountability conversations. In this section, feedback and accountability are explored as well as the value of feedback to the leader.

Great employees need feedback too, especially when they are promoted. There is no way employees will ever reach their true potential unless the leader is willing to have effective conversations that provide guidance and hold them accountable. In the busy lives of many professionals, these conversations easily fall to the wayside. You may assume the right people really don't need the feedback and accountability. But they do. Decide to hold these conversations routinely and use information in this section to figure out 'How' to make it routine.

With the determination to become more effective at accountability and delivering feedback, let's explore 'How,' not 'If' to get it done, one step at a time.

I Am Fine the Way I Am

You need to change! Don't you cringe when someone says, or even implies, that you need to change? It is human nature, and in fact, crucial to our well-being, that we think highly of ourselves. However, this leads to a natural resistance to the thought that we need to change ourselves.

Just the Way They Are
As a manager, when delivering feedback about something you would like the employee to change, focus on the employee's behaviors, not their personality traits. Instead of talking about their bad attitude, speak about their inappropriate approach. People are not able to change 'the way they are'. They are only able to change their behaviors. Some people are more easily excitable and upset than others. Telling that person to "not get upset" is completely ineffective. It's their natural reaction.

For example, an employee who yells at a customer has been rude, no doubt. However, telling that employee they need to stop being rude makes them defensive and puts them in a difficult *and ambiguous* position.

First, their understanding of rude may not be the same as yours. You risk a change to a behavior that is still unacceptable. Secondly, we rarely know how to change what we consider to be 'just how we are'. This employee may see her/himself as being perfectly appropriate given the situation.

Focus on Behaviors

Instead, if the manager speaks to the employee about their inappropriate approach to the customer, they leave the conversation open for discussion. At this point, the manager begins to brainstorm with the employee for more appropriate and detailed actions the employee could have taken. The manager may discuss the boundaries:

- Under no circumstances do we ever yell at a customer,

- meeting customer expectations is very important, and

- your satisfaction as an employee is also crucial.

Then, they begin to discuss what other behaviors the employee may utilize given a similar situation:

- Ask clarifying questions,

- restate the areas where you and the customer agree,

- take a deep breath,

- step away for a moment to 'check on something' to compose yourself, and

- seek the assistance of a manager once you have tried all these approaches.

These examples of appropriate behaviors all give the employee something concrete to think about. These are changes in behavior the employee can put into action as opposed to changing him/herself. No employee likes to hear about their weaknesses, but they may be willing to hear about skills in need of improvement. Handling customers is a skill that can be developed through experience, modeling, mentoring and training.

Instead of telling an employee, "you're too pushy", clarify what you mean. You may actually be trying to tell them to, "listen for the other person's point of view and ask questions in order to arrive at a conclusion that works for all involved."

Developing Skills and Abilities

Employees will be much more receptive to constructive criticism when they feel you are helping them to develop skills and abilities as opposed to trying to change who they are. This may at first seem like a small detail or just a matter of wording, but it is in fact a very powerful approach. When you look carefully at the words that you use, you are also forcing yourself as the supervisor to define what behaviors really are appropriate. This is often a challenge that we leave up to the employee if we approach the situation from the personality standpoint.

Remember, the goal is to improve behavior,
not to personally attack the employee!

Reading inspires thought.
Thought leads to ideas.
Ideas generate action.
Action happens one step at a time.
The first step is the most difficult
to determine and to take.

What are the first steps you will take as a result of reading this article?

1. _____
2. _____
3. _____

Be Critical!

Be Critical, but be Specific.
There is nothing wrong with being critical of your employees' performance. Demand top performance, demand increased productivity, demand awesome customer service and demand they take initiative! But, be very specific about the desired end result and how the company values (*how* we do business) apply to this situation. Be sure of what you want and specifically describe it.

Diagnose the problem behaviors with the employee.
Ask them what they think. Don't accept, "I don't know" as an answer. Tell them that you believe they can help to come up with a solution. Clearly describe what increased productivity or taking initiative looks like and ask what they think they could do differently to achieve that picture.

Don't accept mediocre performance.
Describe specifically what you want. Be critical when it doesn't happen, and reiterate specifically what you want to happen instead.

Reward good performance and small steps toward it.
After describing specifically what you want, acknowledge with a brief conversation when the desirable behavior has occurred. Acknowledge effort, small successes and significant improvement.

Demand that every employee is part of your top performing team!

Reading inspires thought.
Thought leads to ideas.
Ideas generate action.
Action happens one step at a time.
The first step is the most difficult
to determine and to take.

What are the first steps you will take as a result of reading this article?

1. _____
2. _____
3. _____

Miracles Will Not Happen on Their Own

Think about an employee who has a performance problem. They don't do things the way you want them to. You consider whether or not they will make it in the organization. A year from now, they probably won't still be an employee of the company.

If you have one of these employees, you decide whether to address or to ignore their behavior. If you address it, it will either improve, or you will be much more certain it won't improve and you will feel confident about terminating the employee. If you don't address it, their behavior will either stay the same or get worse. *They will not get better on their own.* This is because *better* means that their performance is more in line with *your expectations, which they cannot understand more clearly without your help.*

If they are technically competent, they are probably not meeting your expectations for one of two reasons. Either because they:

1 – do not understand what you want, or

2 – do not agree with you. In this case, they need to have a discussion to convince themselves, or put it in their frame of reference, so they can buy in.

If they are a relatively new hire, rarely are they absolutely not able to do the job unless your interviewing process is very poor. If they are open to improving their performance with effective coaching from you, they can achieve success.

Address the two reasons:

1. You may need to clarify your expectations. You may want to write them down or clarify what's written.

2. You need to get the employee to talk. Hearing you explain *again* won't do it. Get the employee to talk about what their performance needs to look like, what they are going to do to get there, what obstacles they face and what you can do to help (in that order). If they don't agree with your expectations, consciously or subconsciously, they need to have a dialog with you so you can determine if they are both able and willing to change.

Remember – if you don't address an unacceptable behavior, there is a snowball's chance in the Memphis summer that they will change on their own!

Reading inspires thought.
Thought leads to ideas.
Ideas generate action.
Action happens one step at a time.
The first step is the most difficult
to determine and to take.

What are the first steps you will take as a result of reading this article?

1. _____

2. _____

3. _____

Are you Predictable?

As an innovative leader, you may run from predictability. But, your employees and customers love it. Predictability does not mean that you do not innovate; they are not mutually exclusive. Innovation enables the business to thrive through positive changes and maintains competitiveness. Predictability makes employees and customers feel comfortable so they continue to work for you, and do business with you, throughout times of growth and change.

Can your employees predict their success? Can your customers predict their satisfaction and the product they will receive?

What in your company guarantees reliability? **Systems**.

How do you know if they are working? **Measurement**.

A Good Employee System:

- Sets expectations in well written job descriptions which match what you expect, demand and for what you hold them accountable.

- Evaluates performance and success through systematic, routine coaching and evaluations at least yearly.

Measure results so you know if it's working:

- Measure the specific results you detailed in the job description that are expected of the employee. Have them report to you on their current performance on key metrics and progress on important action items.

A Good Customer System:

- Produces a reliable product or service.

- Produces reliable interaction.

- Delivers results.

Measure results so you know if it's working:

- Identify metrics that measure the quality, reliability and consistency of your product or service.

- Track when customers return, if they increase the business they do with you, and when they refer you new business.

As you grow and innovate as all good leaders do, make sure your employees and customers have some predictability so they stick around!

Reading inspires thought.
Thought leads to ideas.
Ideas generate action.
Action happens one step at a time.
The first step is the most difficult
to determine and to take.

What are the first steps you will take as a result of reading this article?

1. _____
2. _____
3. _____

What Gets Measured, Gets Done

"What gets measured gets done!" This is a common truth in large and small businesses, teams and work groups. Measuring success, or progress toward a goal, is incredibly important to achieving the desired ends. Goal gurus tell us that goals need to be SMART - Specific, Measurable, Achievable, Results Oriented and Time-Oriented.

Being able to measure your goals allows you to know how much you've progressed, and how much you have left to do. What remains to be accomplished, given its urgency and importance, will help you to prioritize, and decide what needs to be done today, tomorrow, this week and this month.

Share Information
Even if you diligently measure your progress, adjust your efforts and address challenges that arise, you may not be sharing this information with your whole team. Their individual role in the organization will determine what information is relevant to each person.

We all like to see the revenue dollars increasing, the return on each project reach targets, the pile on our desk decrease and deadlines be met. Employees are no different and need to hear how the company is doing. Particularly in small companies, the employees feel a part of all that is happening and need to hear the successes and the challenges.

Celebrate Success

Celebrating success gives everyone a boost of energy and acknowledging shortcomings gives everyone in the company a common focus. Companies often give bonuses when goals are met, but do nothing when they are not. This creates a giant silent void when they are not doing well and employees wonder, "What can *we* do to bring that bonus back?"

At the beginning of each quarter is a great time to stop and review progress:

1. Pull out your company and department goals. Double-check that each one has a component that can be measured.

2. Measure your success year-to-date on each goal.

3. Share that information with your whole team as appropriate to their role in the company - ensuring everyone hears information on progress.

4. Share with each person what they can do to contribute to the success of each goal. Ask for their input as to how they can positively affect progress.

5. Tell them when you will be sharing the next status report. If possible, give them access to the data so they can determine their individual numbers and report to you. This should happen at least monthly, if not more often. If you are finding it difficult based on the measures you are using, find additional measures that can be reviewed weekly or monthly.

6. Your team will focus on what you measure. Require employees to measure and report their progress to you and to the team according to key metrics they should be watching related to their individual performance.

Know how your company is doing and share the good and the bad news! It will help motivate your employees, build loyalty and increase your success.

Reading inspires thought.
Thought leads to ideas.
Ideas generate action.
Action happens one step at a time.
The first step is the most difficult
to determine and to take.

What are the first steps you will take as a result of reading this article?

1. _____
2. _____
3. _____

Delegating – Must it be so Difficult?

Why, yes – delegating is a painful process. Think about it. You delegate what you have been doing yourself and now want someone else to do. And at some point, we have all murmured: "If you want something done right, do it yourself."

I'd Rather Not Manage Employees, Thanks.

Why must you do things yourself? Why are you so busy? Why does it sound so easy, but is so hard, to delegate? You may have convinced yourself that you do not mind stepping in and doing some tasks yourself just to get them done and get them done right.

Managers often do tasks themselves, because quite honestly; they'd prefer not to manage people. Yes, employees are great when they do tasks on their own. When they perform poorly, the manager may put up with it for a time and then decide to complete the tasks themselves.

It's not easy to interact with people. That's the bottom line. Only a small percentage of the population is similar to you. The rest require significant effort to interact with successfully.

A major difference between businesses that simply continue to exist and those that are successful, is the ability of the manager to get the employees to do what they want and need them to do. Are you connecting with your employees? Are they doing what you want them to do? Or are you tweaking what you want and expect from them based on what they are able to do without much intervention and management from you?

Why is it so Difficult to Delegate?

There are two main reasons:

1. *You must communicate expectations.* Before you decide to delegate, you are doing the task yourself to your standards. When you do it yourself, your expectations are clearly communicated – you don't need to explain your expectations to yourself. You tend to give yourself credit for your strengths and quickly correct any mistakes. If it's not done timely, you already know the reasons why and may give yourself the benefit of the doubt. This is all human nature. It is much more difficult to communicate expectations to *someone else,* learn where someone else is coming from and help them to improve their performance.

2. *You must hold the delegate-ee accountable.* Typically, one of the most difficult things a manager must

do is to hold others accountable. And this is a task often avoided and ignored by managers. If you do not hold the delegate-ee accountable, chances are you will see poor results or end up doing the task yourself once again.

How do you delegate effectively?

1. Determine what tasks, responsibilities or decisions you wish to delegate.

2. Decide how you expect things to be done. Clarify your expectations and the results you desire.

3. Choose the right person.

4. Check they possess the necessary skills and abilities.

5. Communicate your expectations, boundaries and deadlines. Ensure they understand what you are explaining and do not assume they understand.

6. Transfer Responsibility. Make sure they realize they have become responsible for the task and the results.

7. Hold the delegate-ee accountable on a set schedule you determined at the time of delegation. Follow up to ensure the task is being done right.

8. If it needs to be redone; re-explain, teach, counsel if necessary and reinforce expectations.

> **Do not do the task yourself,** and do not assume responsibility back from the employee.

9. Reward good performance, and coach or counsel poor performance.

Delegating requires you transfer your expectations from your brain to the delegate-ee; you stick with them as they work through the task and you hold them accountable for great performance. That's difficult!

Reading inspires thought.
Thought leads to ideas.
Ideas generate action.
Action happens one step at a time.
The first step is the most difficult
to determine and to take.

What are the first steps you will take as a result of reading this article?

1. _____
2. _____
3. _____

Right Back at 'cha!

Feedback to the boss

Effective evaluations are a critical avenue to provide employees with valuable feedback to focus their attention and energy, build upon their strengths and address areas where they may be falling below your expectations.

Have you ever asked for feedback from your employees to help *you* to focus, build on *your* strengths and address *your* problem areas? The interactions and relationships you have with your employees are a critical component of your success. Many unhappy employees do not complain. And often those with ideas may not come forward, at least not with ideas that may appear critical of the way you do things. The employees' happiness is linked to their performance, which is heavily linked to your bottom line results.

How to Ask for Feedback
You need to determine how to obtain employee feedback. There are several different ways to consider:

1. You can ask them directly by opening a staff meeting discussion to their comments and suggestions.

2. You can use a mid-level manager or outside facilitator to elicit your employees' comments about you as their manager.

3. You can give employees a feedback questionnaire with open ended questions for them to answer.

4. You can use an anonymous 360-degree survey tool, often conducted online.

Many leaders have received insightful feedback by using a questionnaire (#3). Even more accurate input and comprehensive feedback can be obtained by conducting an anonymous 360-degree assessment (#4). The survey results give you feedback in a variety of specific areas and open ended questions obtain input in more general areas.

It's important to remember that while you call the shots as the manager, employee input is very valuable. Once you obtain the feedback, take the time to respond and address issues identified. This does not mean that you must immediately deliver upon all their requests. But, don't forget their requests. It is important to remember that *whatever they said, it was important enough to them to say.* Look for their message and address that; even if you can't immediately fix the problem they've identified.

Reading inspires thought.
Thought leads to ideas.
Ideas generate action.
Action happens one step at a time.
The first step is the most difficult
to determine and to take.

What are the first steps you will take as a result of reading this article?

1. _____
2. _____
3. _____

Rating Scales in Evaluations?

When you use a rating scale in an evaluation, of course every employee wants a '5' on all variables. The problem is that once they are scored at a '5', you communicate that they have no more room for improvement. If you don't give them a '5', they are worried about what their raise will be (if the evaluation is the main tool used to determine their raise), so they often argue about the number. No one wants less than a '3', because then the message is, "You stink!" So, consider how much you can tell an employee about their performance by rating them with a '3' or a '4'. The fact is that a rating scale can deliver a snapshot of performance, but does not provide any significant, specific or usable feedback.

Often a rating scale is associated with a predetermined definition of each of the numbers. This allows for uniformity among the evaluators, but gives the evaluator an excuse not to add narrative feedback. Detailed, specific feedback is what causes an evaluation to facilitate real changes in performance rather than simply being a tool to determine raises with no focus on actual improvement.

You may ask, "Well, if I can't use a rating scale, how do I give an effective evaluation?"

Think about what you are trying to achieve. As a manager, you want to improve your employees' performance in order to achieve your business goals. You also want to help your employees to feel good about the job they are doing, learn new skills and improve their overall personal and professional performance.

In order to do so in an evaluation, you must give specific, detailed feedback which they are able to directly apply to their daily actions, changing their behavior and leading to better results.

First, give the employee specific examples of their excellent performance, and then give specific examples of behaviors that need improvement. Describe exactly what results you want to see that you haven't been seeing. Talk to them about these aspects of their job and get their input. *Together* determine specific behaviors they need to add, change or tweak in order to improve their outcomes. Do this for each aspect of their job.

It may sound easy, but this requires significant effort on your part to look at each aspect of their job, track good and bad behaviors and put it all together come evaluation time. Giving useful, applicable feedback is not easy, but is worth every moment you spend doing it.

Make the Process Easier

A few things can make this process easier. Keep their job description near you every day and when you see something positive or negative, write notes next to the applicable job duty directly on the job description. The picture you paint with this information at evaluation time will be specific, comprehensive and helpful to them.

Group tasks when you evaluate. Employees don't need detailed, specific feedback on every single job duty. Certain duties build off one another and are logically combined for evaluation purposes.

Very few employees will admit to enjoying feedback, especially critical comments. However, when it helps them to tweak their performance and experience greater success, they'll come back ready for more!

Reading inspires thought.
Thought leads to ideas.
Ideas generate action.
Action happens one step at a time.
The first step is the most difficult
to determine and to take.

What are the first steps you will take as a result of reading this article?

1. _____
2. _____
3. _____

Top Five Criteria for Successful Performance Evaluations

1. Use a form that makes sense.

2. Require employee input.

3. Document very specific examples.

4. Use metrics to support your feedback.

5. Obtain commitment to do something differently.

The best performance evaluations are those that directly evaluate based on the tasks in the job description instead of rating employees from '1' to '5' on vague characteristics like initiative. Regardless of what form you are required to use, start by looking at the employee's job tasks, identifying specific things they do well and areas in which they need to focus or improve. Brainstorm for specific examples of situations that demonstrate both their successes and their challenges. This feedback can be used on any form.

The employee should also evaluate themselves in order to identify opportunities for their professional development. Have them complete the same evaluation form you are going to use. Or ask them to email you five specific examples of situations where they were successful and three specific examples of situations that pinpoint where they would like to improve their performance. Give them a deadline early enough so you are able to send it back to them if it needs more detail.

The chain of events to obtain employee input:

1. You give the employee an evaluation form with a deadline of 48 hours to enter their input. Encourage them to point out their own specific successes to take credit for them!

2. You draft your evaluation feedback.

3. They turn in their evaluation with specific examples of successes as well as situations that did not go so well.

4. They pinpoint three areas where they would like to focus on improving over the next year.

5. You compare their input and your feedback and add their input to your form (the official one) as needed, becoming aware of where you might disagree significantly with the employee.

6. You deliver feedback using your copy, and file their self evaluation feedback in their file.

If their job is based on a lot of numbers, that gives you objective measurement of performance. Beyond the numbers, and *to support the numbers*, you offer your specific examples of when they did well; in other words, what they did to create the good numbers they have or how they handled a customer situation well. Do the same thing for the less desirable numbers.

The specific examples are what make the numbers come alive and become more personal. Metrics on their own may not tell the whole story, but talking through what makes the numbers what they are, how the employee contributes to the numbers and over what they have control will be significant.

Then, choose no more than four or five areas where you would like them to focus during the next 6-12 months (until the next evaluation). These may be areas where they are strong and have ability to improve even more. These could be areas where they are failing miserably and need to get on track, or areas where you see greater potential than what they are currently achieving. Maybe they are scared to make mistakes or scared to push out of their comfort zone. These are not four or five tasks. They are areas broad enough to provide focus for 6-12 months. Each month or quarter, you spend time with the employee to identify the specific tasks they will do to make progress on these broad areas.

You determine these areas to improve based on your observations combined with their input. Then, the employee comes up with specific action items that they will implement in the next 30-90 days to make progress on these areas. The specific action items must be what they will *do differently.* Trying harder will not cut it. They should determine the action items with your coaching assistance, and sincerely buy in and commit to them.

Reading inspires thought.
Thought leads to ideas.
Ideas generate action.
Action happens one step at a time.
The first step is the most difficult
to determine and to take.

What are the first steps you will take as a result of reading this article?

1. _____
2. _____
3. _____

Top 5 Mistakes Leaders Make Promoting from Within

James was a great employee. He was the perfect choice for the management opening. His talents and skills, his focus on results and his expertise with customers and systems, all made him a great choice for the promotion. Why then, is he doing such a terrible job as a manager? Did you make the wrong choice?

Too often, leaders forget that a promotion to management requires a major transition. It requires going from being great at what they do, to taking on a whole new set of tasks and measuring their own success in completely different ways. They lose their peers who they knew and liked and gain employees from whom they need to keep a distance. It is a traumatic experience. Do you have a manager in a situation like James? Are you there to help them through it?

The Top Five Mistakes leaders make in the transition of their star employees to managers:

Assumed their tactical expertise would directly translate into management expertise.

Many leaders have their own story of how they were thrown into a management role and had to figure it out the hard way. Some survive that way and some don't. Internal promotions often assume that the person has more knowledge about the bigger picture or that the expectations from above are more clear than they really are.

Solution: Create a complete training outline. Every new role, whether it is for a new employee or a promoted employee, should be prefaced with a training outline. This is the list of things that they need to know in order to be successful in the new position, when they will be taught, when they will be expected to know/ master each area, and what mastery looks like. If there are things that they already know, they should still be included in the list, verified and can be quickly checked off.

Failed to teach them the management skills necessary to thrive.

Managing people requires they understand how to create and communicate expectations, connect with their direct reports, inspire them to do well, and engage them in productive accountability discussions. These are not natural skills to most individuals and must be learned and then coached consistently over time by their supervisor.

Solution: Do an honest inventory of these skills, and plan to help them to learn more in the areas which they are weak. Provide books and resources, the opportunity for a mentor and key leadership relationships, classes or a leadership coach, and personally teach in areas in which you excel. Don't ignore a lack of skills that you have noticed from their time as an employee! Use that information.

Did not set your expectations clearly.

There is an incredibly long distance from what is in your head to what comes out of your mouth. Your new manager cannot read your mind. There are many things you may expect that you have never clearly outlined or discussed, even if you have worked with them for some time. "Improve morale" may mean one thing to you and something quite different to the promoted manager.

Solution: Clarify your expectations. Ask yourself:

- What are the most important tasks that they will do?

- What results do you expect they will achieve?

- How would you like them to do the job? Specify only details necessary to keep them focused, and give them room to do it their way.

- What have other managers done that you do not like and wish the new manager would not do?

- What deadlines will you put on each of these expectations and how you will measure whether or not they have been successful?

Offered no accountability.

Even the best employee who takes initiative and tries their hardest will not thrive without some degree of feedback and a requirement to report back to their manager. This step is critical but is often seen as unimportant, especially if you already know this person is a star employee. In order to meet your expectations and company goals, they must receive input about what they are achieving and where they are falling short. If delivered along the way, they have time to tweak their performance, not just to fail or survive in the end. If you don't provide feedback, yet let them continue to under-perform, shame on you! If you don't provide feedback in the areas they are doing well, don't expect that behavior to continue!

Solution: Provide routine, expected, conversational feedback. Set a routine conversation with a set agenda (of focus areas, new skills to learn, tasks to perfect, action items, successes, and challenges). The conversation is scheduled, the appointment is kept and the newly promoted manager is expected to be the one to prepare for and report on the agenda you have set.

You never asked them to think.
Transition to management can be a traumatic one. Suddenly, they are in charge and powerful, yet they've lost their peers and their comfort zone. They are no

longer rewarded for doing the tasks they are good at, but expected to think strategically and develop other people. Management is about accomplishing results, using processes in place, improving them as necessary, solving problems and developing people. If they are not thinking, you are in trouble.

Solution: Get them to think.   Getting them to think requires that you set the direction, ask questions and get them talking about how they see the situation, possible solutions and approaches, and why they will choose the avenue they choose. Too often a manager of managers still wants to be the one to solve the problems even though they have a manager to lead the team to solve a problem. Thinking through a situation can be facilitated greatly by a leader who asks the right questions instead of giving the solution. You want your new manager to be independent, so ask them the questions and get them to think!

What mistakes have you made when promoting someone to management? What have you done right?

Reading inspires thought.
Thought leads to ideas.
Ideas generate action.
Action happens one step at a time.
The first step is the most difficult
to determine and to take.

What are the first steps you will take as a result of reading this article?

1. _____

2. _____

3. _____

HOW not *IF*

Goals
Section Overview

Setting goals without a clear understanding of what's really important to you can be a laborious task and your goals may not be consistently realized. Spend time determining your passion, then be disciplined enough to write your goals. Make it a routine process every year and every quarter. Decide 'How' it will happen, not 'If' it will this year. Don't keep them to yourself. Engage your team! This section's articles offer guidance on how to identify your passion, write effective goals and make consistent progress *every* day!

Identifying your passion and setting goals is critical to successfully navigating difficult conversations because they form the basis, the focus and the potential common ground in a conversation. Preferences, opinions and feelings can all cloud a conversation, but agreed upon goals and values bring people together and facilitate good conversations.

With the determination to become focused on goals, let's explore 'How,' not 'If' to get it done, one step at a time.

Finding Your Passion

Have you written financial, operational, sales and marketing, and personal goals this year? Have you started thinking about next year?

There is a secret to accomplishing these goals, and that is to *want* to achieve them. In order to really desire to achieve a goal, it must in some way be linked to those things about which you are passionate. Many professionals crank out work on a daily basis and never really discover where their passion lies.

It is a lifelong journey to discover and refine those things about which you are passionate, and it needs to start right away. *One important thing to remember about finding your passion is that it most certainly is... All about YOU!* What is deep inside you is a powerful driving force for your success.

Consider pondering the answers to these questions in a quiet moment or with a trusted peer group. The answers to these questions will lead you to the core of your passions.

Whom do you admire?

These people may or may not be famous, close to you, or even have done something anyone else would think is significant. What do *you* admire about them?

What is important to you?

What are the things that really get under your skin; things that you feel are just not right? Why does this bother you? What does this tell you about what is important to you? How does that translate to your daily work?

What do you value?

Can you choose the top five things you value out of this list, even if they are all relatively important?

1. Innovation - continuous improvement of processes and products

2. Consistency – producing the same dependable results

3. Reliability – predictability according to set expectations

4. Phenomenal Customer Service

5. Accuracy – precision and details

6. Client's Personal Improvement

7. "Wow" Work – consistent client response

8. Cleanliness – of locations and equipment

9. Productivity – maximum utilization of resources

10. Efficiency – in planning, production

11. Punctuality and Timeliness – as promised, on time, hit deadlines

12. Quality – function, speed, value, suitability

13. Responsiveness – reaction to customer needs, and anticipated needs

14. Safety – of products, services, and facilities

15. Speed – replies, production, changes

16. Accountability – of the team for performance and results

17. Communication – proactive, frequent, according to preferences, effective

18. Cooperation – among individuals and departments

19. Competition – strive to excel, exceed performance levels of the past or of others

20. Coordination – seamless interaction of individuals and stakeholders

21. Discipline – adherence to policies, procedures, systems, schedules and standards

22. Risk taking – ability of employees to take risks, make decisions, and try new things

23. Systemization – creation of systems and processes to streamline operations

24. Professional development – improvement by all individuals, departments and company as a whole

25. Creativity – bright ideas, connecting the seemingly unrelated ideas and concepts

26. Integrity – doing what you say you will do, behind the scenes as well

27. Solid relationships – with employees, vendors, partners

28. Giving back to the community – with employee time, donations, projects

When have you felt most happy, enthusiastic and successful?
What is it about that situation that you really like?

What do you enjoy most about vacations, holidays, or events - both routine daily events and large significant events?
Each person looks at the same situation a little bit differently and you can learn what really motivates you by looking at regular situations.

What are your goals, and why?
Why are these things important to you? Why *now*?

What do your employees or coworkers do that really annoys you?
What would you prefer they did instead? Why?

Every one of these questions could be a week of thought in the mountains. Taking just a bit of time to get started can be a very valuable step on the journey to finding your passion!

Reading inspires thought.
Thought leads to ideas.
Ideas generate action.
Action happens one step at a time.
The first step is the most difficult
to determine and to take.

What are the first steps you will take as a result of reading this article?

1. _____

2. _____

3. _____

Your Vision is the Picture of your Competitive Edge

Your competitive edge creates sustained profits by producing value. What is it about how you do business that makes you different? Do you have a cost advantage that enables you to offer a product or service cheaper - maybe because you have a unique supplier, efficient manufacturing process, or less overhead? Do you have a differentiation advantage that enables you to offer benefits that exceed what your customers can find elsewhere? Does this differentiation come from your operational abilities, processes and systems, proprietary know-how, customer service, reputation, patents and trademarks, ability to innovate or ability to be efficient and produce superior quality?

All that is important. What really has the potential to differentiate you from your competition and influences all of the above advantages is your vision - your unique way of doing business. As the famous scientist, Buckminster Fuller once told a young boy, "No one looks at the world exactly as you do!"

Don't be fooled into believing that your vision is the same as your skills or strengths. Skills are what you are good at, strengths are what energize you. Your strengths are much more likely what will allow you to achieve great success in your business and play a more vital role in your vision. Skills can be learned.

Defining your Vision

How do you know what makes you unique? Spend some time on these two activities:

1. On a tough day, make a list of what bugs you. Then ask yourself why. Look for your deep seated values that translate into how you want to do business. Which of these values are most important to you?

   For example, it really bugs me when an employee does not know how to solve a problem and doesn't care to search for a solution. Why does that bother *me?* Well, not really because the problem isn't solved. What really bothers *me* is that the employee is not pushing themselves, is not learning something new, and is leaving much of their potential undiscovered.

2. You are going on vacation for two months to Costa Rica to enjoy the beaches, the mountains, the white water rafting and the hot springs. The good news is that it is an all-expense-paid trip. The challenge is that you are not allowed to communicate with anyone back at the office. However, you must ensure that your operations continue to function how you want them to, so

you still have happy customers and employees when you return. What guidance will you leave?

This guidance must be specific enough to help them to know and understand the criteria you use to make decisions. You cannot simply say, "Do what I would do." Write this guidance to let them know what it is you would do.

Whether you are an owner, C-level executive or manager within an organization, your individual vision is what has the opportunity to bring great success to your team. Within an organization, your vision must be in line with the company vision. However, the critical difference is that your vision as a manager is *how* you wish your team to operate in order to meet expected results and accomplish company objectives. While respecting the company vision and mission, policies, procedures and systems, there is still plenty of room for your passion and vision to guide how your team will operate. When you access that passion and vision, your team has a much greater chance of meeting and exceeding the company goals.

What to Do With It

Once you determine what is important to you, what do you do with it?

1. Name it

   a. Values, Guiding principles, Mission/Vision, Competitive Advantage

2. Verify it

    a. Check profit routinely. Make sure you have narrowed it down enough that you don't look like everyone else. "Customer Service is our first priority," is way too common to be a competitive edge.

3. Document it

    a. Writing something on paper provides a sanity check, adds clarity and means a whole lot more coming across to others.

    b. Add to Job descriptions and Evaluation forms.

4. Implement it

    a. Check all processes against these standards

    b. Share it. It probably won't be a surprise to your team, but seeing it in organized form will be powerful.

5 Expand upon it

    a. Grow with your strengths.

    b. When you hire, they must fit.

6. Preserve it. Hang on to it like a tiger on a piece of meat.

    a. If it seems to evaporate, go find it again - maybe in a new form.

What is unique about the way *you* do business?

Reading inspires thought.
Thought leads to ideas.
Ideas generate action.
Action happens one step at a time.
The first step is the most difficult
to determine and to take.

What are the first steps you will take as a result of reading this article?

1. _____
2. _____
3. _____

Egotistical Jerk or Passionate Leader?

If you've ever had the boss who has said,

- "My way or the highway!"
- "...because I said so!"
- "That's just the way it is," and
- "Get it done yesterday - I don't care how!"

you may be hesitant to come across like a demanding jerk to *your* employees.

So, *when* do you get tough and lay it on the line, even to the point of saying, "That's just how it is!" to your employees?

You know you're being a jerk when...

1. There is a self-serving motive behind your rant like ego preservation, desire to win/they lose, or desire to intimidate.

2. You do not take the time to let them speak.

3. You honestly don't care what they think and don't feel like they can contribute more than you already know despite their subject matter expertise.

You know you are being a passionate leader when...

1. You listen curiously and with genuine interest to what they are saying, combining empathy with high standards.

2. Your blood pressure starts to rise because they have/or continue to do something hurtful to accomplishing the company vision, mission, or goals.

3. You respond carefully and choose your words to avoid being hurtful *and* present the mission and vision components with passion because that is the reason why their behavior is a problem.

You **can** get excited and passionate about your core values, vision, mission and goals.

You **cannot** scream and yell because someone made you mad and has frustrated you.

You **can** get determined and definite when what an employee did interfered with overall accomplishment of goals or was contrary to the way you want your company or department to operate.

You **cannot** get miffed, sarcastic and rude because someone kept you personally from meeting your goal.

The mission, vision and core values of an organization are its backbone, the reason it exists and how business should be conducted. This backbone is a reason to be excited and no one will fault you if you are passionate and determined about it, as long as you treat them respectfully (no yelling, swearing, sarcasm, personal attacks or demeaning comments). You may even appear egotistical if you are personally very invested in the core values and vision. But a drive toward an admirable vision is always about more than just your desire to be personally successful, and that will come through to your team.

Reading inspires thought.
Thought leads to ideas.
Ideas generate action.
Action happens one step at a time.
The first step is the most difficult
to determine and to take.

What are the first steps you will take as a result of reading this article?

1. _____

2. _____

3. _____

Writing and Achieving Goals

If you don't know where you want to go, you'll probably never get there.

Are you Drowning?

> *"You don't drown by falling in the water;*
> *you drown by staying there!"*
> *- Edwin Louis Cole*

It is said that if a frog is placed in boiling water, it will jump out, but if it is placed in cool water that is slowly heated, it will never jump out and will be boiled alive.

What are you doing in your business that you need to wake up and change?

Change is difficult and it's almost impossible to travel from here to there if you don't know where 'here' is and where 'there' is. If I told you to figure out how to go from Manjimup to Pemberton and both towns were in Australia, chances are you would have a hard time doing it without using maps. With a basic map of Australia, even without knowing road names, you could tell me to drive North to Perth, fly to Adelaide and then drive North to Pemberton. Then we could work on the details. Goals are the map for your team!

Is your team being slowly heated in hot water, are they driving themselves insane and are they staying in the water when they don't know how to swim?

From Here to There...

Where are you now? You can't decide what to change if you don't measure your performance on multiple key variables, key performance indicators, or metrics. And, there is more to the picture than those numbers. You also must track the key activities that you are routinely completing to achieve the performance metrics you achieve – bad and good. With these *two* pieces of information you can decide how and what to change.

Then you must determine where you want to be. That requires writing solid goals for the year and breaking them into action items for this month, this week and today. You may want to do the 'If...then' exercise to add some clarity. Instead of, "I want to grow," try, "If I grow to a $2M company, then I could... *or* we could... *or* it would mean that..." You must have something concrete to strive for in order for you and your team to make leaps.

Do you have written goals for this year?

Top Excuses for not Writing Goals

5. They are already in my head, very clearly.

4. I can't predict the future; I'm just going to keep working extra hard all year.

3. If I write them down on paper, and don't reach them...I'll have failed!

2. This year we survived and even thrived, we will just keep doing the same things.

1. Things work best when I go with my gut in the moment

Effective Goals

1. Commit to write them.

2. Write them well.

3. Share them.

Steps to Writing Effective Goals

1. Write a list of the Top 50 things you most want to accomplish in the upcoming 12 months, include personal and professional aspirations. *This is the hardest part – get it done and you are well on your way.* These are not yet goals; these are all the things you want to accomplish - optimistically, unrealistically, enthusiastically, and ideally.

2. Group them into categories of related topics to focus your efforts.

3. Identify the top three items that you are most *excited about.*

4. Choose 5-10 items which you want to turn into goals. Rewrite them as SMART goals, Specific, Measurable, Achievable, Realistic and Time-oriented (have a deadline for completion).

5. Identify and acknowledge the two which will be most difficult to achieve. *Are your goals ambitious?* Do they reflect where you really want to be or simply what you will settle for? Ask yourself if you've reached a bit with these goals. Have you set them based on what *you* want to achieve, or what you think your industry or your business is comfortably capable of?

6. Take the end-of-period goal and break it into what you need to achieve each quarter and month in order to reach the end-of-period goal.

A majority of leaders do not write a complete list of goals. Many only have a revenue number goal or a list of goals their boss generated. What each leader wants to accomplish is very important in addition to what the company expects. You don't need to write goals in order to stay employed, but your chances of achieving great success in your role is much better if you clarify your goals enough to write them and write them clearly enough to share them with those on your team.

Are your Goals a Secret?

Who else knows about them? Have you told an accountability partner about your goals so they can occasionally ask you how it's going?

Do you need help achieving your goals? Have you engaged your team? Do your employees know what your goals are? Do those who work for you know where the business is headed and what they have to look forward to by the end of the year? If you've created some ambitious goals, phenomenal performance by your employees is integral for you to reach those milestones that you really want to accomplish! They cannot be part of your success if they don't know where you are heading.

Seriously look at the goals you've written or the goals you've been delegated. Look at the strategies you've identified to achieve each goal. What role do each of your team members need to play and who else is important to achieving these goals? Have you shared the goals with your employees and determined and explained what you expect from them? Not all goals may involve all team members, so share those that are pertinent.

Whatever you hope to achieve, be careful not to expect to do it all yourself. You may be able to, but it is rarely the best idea. Challenge your employees, discover their potential, set clear expectations that encourage them to get involved, and excite them with a sense of accomplishment for playing a role in the company's growth and success.

Don't keep your goals a secret! Know whose help you need, share the goals with them, determine their role and get them excited to be part of the success!

What would your employees say if I asked them what will be *new, exciting and different* in the business 12 months from now?

Reading inspires thought.
Thought leads to ideas.
Ideas generate action.
Action happens one step at a time.
The first step is the most difficult
to determine and to take.

What are the first steps you will take as a result of reading this article?

1. _____
2. _____
3. _____

New Day's Resolutions

A New Year's Resolution is a funny thing. Individuals seem to either swear by them or run from them. The end of the year is a natural time to look at what you've accomplished and what you hoped to achieve, and set the plan for the new year.

The spirit of a New Year's Resolution is that it is a good time to forgive yourself for what you did not do last year and make a renewed commitment to do something different this year. As important as it is to write goals, in order to be successful, you must focus on each individual day as well.

As a leader, every day you wake up and make a renewed commitment to those who rely on you, whether it be your family, your employees, your clients, your strategic partners, or any of your many connections. Being your best today and doing the most important things today is a powerful approach to impact the future. One of the things leaders often say is, "What do I do *next?*" Even if they have great goals and plans, first and next steps can be a bit difficult to determine.

As each day concludes and each new day begins is a fantastic time to reflect on the changes you want (or need) to make and resolve to follow through on those changes. Waiting a year is way too long, and hoping a new year will miraculously make a resolution happen without fail is unrealistic. However, determining what is most important to accomplish must be based on solid short and long term goals and established values.

So, do not wait until the beginning of a calendar or fiscal year, start tonight with reviewing where you are on the goals you have set and the plan you have put in place, recommit to achievement and make a resolution for tomorrow about what you will do, will do differently, and will commit to make happen – one day at a time.

How do you eat an elephant?
One bite at a time (if you had such an odd urge).

How do you climb a mountain?
One step at a time (much more realistic activity in my opinion).

Reading inspires thought.
Thought leads to ideas.
Ideas generate action.
Action happens one step at a time.
The first step is the most difficult
to determine and to take.

What are the first steps you will take as a result of reading this article?

1. _____
2. _____
3. _____

HOW not IF

Hiring

Section Overview

There are definite steps to follow to hire well. There are also a million excuses for skipping steps. Hiring well takes time. Interviewing requires some difficult conversations with the candidate in order to determine if they fit the job opening. Managing the wrong employees or executing your disciplinary process also takes a lot of time and the conversations are much more difficult. And the cost is incredibly high to fund the revolving door.

Decide not 'If' you should improve your hiring process, but focus on 'How' you can improve given your current strengths and opportunities. The work begins long before the ad is placed. It begins when the leader takes the time to clearly understand the best roles and tasks for each job and determines the criteria necessary to be successful. It seems easy or obvious, but incorrect assumptions are often made in this step of the process.

251

In this section are checklists and examples of how you might improve your hiring process. Take the time to use these resources to take your process to the next level of effectiveness. You might be hiring well and still experiencing turnover. Other articles cover the management of new hires and highlight the importance of that process.

With the determination to become more effective at hiring, let's explore 'How,' not 'If' to get it done, one step at a time.

The Five Essentials of Hiring Well

Determine if you need to hire.
Define what you are trying to accomplish. Can it be accomplished by current employees? Idle time on anyone's part can hurt the morale of the others. Also, even though the pool of applicants may be good, the employee you know and trust is usually a better option if they can handle the tasks.

Determine exactly what you will need this person to do.
Write the job description and include your ideal picture of what is expected to set high expectations when they start. Tell them specifically what they will do in the detailed job description presented upon making the offer.

Interview!
Interview even if they are a highly recommended referral from someone you know well or if they are an internal candidate.

Use interview questions that pull examples from their past experience.

Start each question with, "Tell me about a specific situation where..." Strike "What would you...?" from your interviewing vocabulary. Avoid questions that can be answered with a "Yes" or a "No". Ask each applicant the same questions. Take notes. You will forget the details if you don't. Ask their references these same types of questions.

Have a trusted employee do a second interview.

Give them interview questions to use. Ask a few of the same questions you give to the peer. Create a comfortable environment for the applicant with the employee, and maybe they'll open up and give you a little bit better idea of who they really are. Remember, the better you understand them, the better chance you will have of finding a great fit for the position for which you are hiring.

It's not about finding the perfect person. It's about finding the person who fits the job well.

Reading inspires thought.
Thought leads to ideas.
Ideas generate action.
Action happens one step at a time.
The first step is the most difficult
to determine and to take.

What are the first steps you will take as a result of reading this article?

1. _____
2. _____
3. _____

Why Would You *Ever* Hire the Wrong Person?

Are you as effective as you would like to be when bringing new members on to your team?

What happens when you hire the wrong person?

- The work doesn't get done or doesn't get done right.

- The person hurts the team's motivation and may lower the standards of other employees based on their poor performance.

- The person annoys your customers or seriously fails to delight customers.

- The person takes a lot of your time to train and manage.

*Why, then, would you **ever** hire the wrong person?*

- You never clearly defined what you wanted them to do in the first place.

- You don't have a truly effective interviewing process.

- You want to, and do, hire a go-getter but what you really need is someone who can do routine, detailed work consistently well.

- You hire someone who has the right technical skills but not the personality to interact with customers which is a key part of their job.

- You like the person and want to give them a job – and the rest of your team likes them too.

- You assume the job is easier and requires more basic skills than it actually does.

- Your friend's son or daughter needs a job.

- Your relative or friend needs a job.

Hiring the right person requires that you:

- Very clearly define expectations and tasks for which they are responsible.

- Define what skills and abilities are required to do those tasks.

- Effectively interview for those particular skills and abilities.

- Involve other team members in the interview process as appropriate.

- Hire slowly, fire quickly if you've made a bad choice.

- Set high expectations from Day One, train/orient thoroughly, and give routine feedback.

Reading inspires thought.
Thought leads to ideas.
Ideas generate action.
Action happens one step at a time.
The first step is the most difficult
to determine and to take.

What are the first steps you will take as a result of reading this article?

1. _____
2. _____
3. _____

Messing With Their Lives

When you hire someone you begin to 'mess with their life'. You may rightfully believe that in 95% of cases you are 'messing' with employees' lives in a positive and beneficial way.

Without a doubt, their job is an enormously significant part of most people's lives:

- It's their livelihood,

- it's how they spend approximately one half of their waking hours,

- it's personally & professionally either rewarding or unfulfilling,

- it's how they describe themselves,

- it's part of how they define their self-worth, and

- it affects their emotional and physical health.

This list could go on. For a surprising number of people, there are times when being at work is much more enjoyable than being at home.

For these reasons plus many more, what you do as their manager has a big impact on employees and on their lives, and has the potential to do great things or cause considerable misery.

There is no easy answer about how to 'mess' *well* with employees' lives. It may be helpful to think about questions such as these:

- Are you aware of what type of impact you are having?

- Do you know how employees feel about the job they are doing?

- What type of impact do you *want* to have on your employees?

- As their manager, how much responsibility do you feel you should take for the impact the job has on their lives?

Even though employees may job hop or appear to take their job lightly, where each person works and what they do has incredible potential to shape their self-image, uncover their potential, enable their success and positively affect their life.

Reading inspires thought.
Thought leads to ideas.
Ideas generate action.
Action happens one step at a time.
The first step is the most difficult
to determine and to take.

What are the first steps you will take as a result of reading this article?

1. _____
2. _____
3. _____

The Perfect Person for this Job...

"I just need that perfect person to fill this perfect position, and everything will be great and my life will be much easier." Sound either familiar or far-fetched?

I absolutely believe in the power of hiring the right people for your team. In fact, there is no way to succeed in a business of significant size unless you employ, subcontract or align yourself with the right people. However, if you find yourself saying the statement above, look at what else you could do to ensure your success so it doesn't need to hinge on the perfect person.

There are a multitude of great potential employees. You can increase your new hire's chances for success by more narrowly defining the criteria *essential* for success in this position you want to fill. Then, find the person that meets that essential criteria, train them to learn additional skills and have a system that supports the less necessary abilities.

Creating a team of people who *all* possess the *essential* criteria to contribute significantly to the success of your company is the most important part of hiring. Filling in the gaps with training and consistent support can be much less of a headache than waiting for the perfect person to arrive for the perfect job.

The million dollar question is, "What are the essential criteria for your company or department?"

Reading inspires thought.
Thought leads to ideas.
Ideas generate action.
Action happens one step at a time.
The first step is the most difficult
to determine and to take.

What are the first steps you will take as a result of reading this article?

1. _____
2. _____
3. _____

How Do I Conduct Really Effective Interviews?

First you must establish the essential ingredients for a successful employee. Determine the specific characteristics that are important to the particular job.

Essential Characteristics might include:

Analysis	Integrity
Decision-making	Persuasiveness
Flexibility	Planning
Customer focus	Resilience
Independence	Stress tolerance
Initiative	Technical ability
Leadership	Verbal communication
Ability to work in a team	Written communication

Then, ask questions based on specific examples from their past experience that relate to these characteristics. Past behavior is the *best* predictor of future behavior. If you ask about what they "would" do, you are simply testing their creativity. On the other hand, people often like to talk about their experiences and will have a harder time making up the level of detail to tell you a specific story from their past.

Examples
Instead of asking, "Do you make many errors at work?" say, "Tell me about a specific time you made an error at work and how you corrected it." Then, make sure you hear an answer to the question you asked. If they answer with what they would do, or in general what they have done, ask the question once again, stressing the words, "specific time".

Instead of asking, "How do you interact with customers?" say, "Describe the most difficult customer with whom you have interacted," or "Tell me about a time you were able to make a very difficult customer happy."

Instead of asking, "Do people consider you an honest person?" say, "Tell me about a time you made a mistake. What happened and how did you correct it?" or "Describe a situation where you saw someone doing something dishonest. What did you do?"

Some general questions that are almost always useful

- Tell me specifically what you liked *most* about your last job/supervisor. (2 questions)

- What did you like *least* about your last job/supervisor? (2 questions) What was your least favorite task at your last job? Pursue the specific example that gives you enough information to determine if they will like the tasks in the job for which they are applying.

- What is more important: Quality or Timeliness? Speed or Accuracy? Give me an example of a time you've found that to be true in your work experience.

- Describe the best/worst team with whom you have ever worked. (2 questions)

- Tell me about a time you went above and beyond your supervisor's expectations.

Other Important Points

- Write interview questions. Ask the interview questions you wrote.

- Be persistent and determined to dig up the answers to the questions you've asked. These are not easy questions to answer. Wait for the applicant to answer.

- Keep written notes from the interview.

- Have multiple interviewers/peer interaction.

Reading inspires thought.
Thought leads to ideas.
Ideas generate action.
Action happens one step at a time.
The first step is the most difficult
to determine and to take.

What are the first steps you will take as a result of reading this article?

1. _____
2. _____
3. _____

A Common Pitfall of Interviewing

Have you ever thought that you may interview in order to satisfy *your* needs? I don't mean the need you have to fill the position. Let me explain.

There are very few things less concrete than interviewing. Although there is a world of information and expertise, and a multitude of experts, there is little proven to be foolproof. Employees frequently quit or are fired, or need to be fired. It may not quite be the "crapshoot" that a client described it as, but for many managers it is far from a science.

When we interact with another person, we are looking for certain dynamics that make us feel good, and then we enjoy the conversation. There are things that each of us likes others to say, ways we want them to approach the conversation and a level of frankness or diplomacy that we want to exist in the conversation. If you say you hire by gut feeling, you may be looking for someone that makes you feel happy or comfortable, not necessarily the best person for the job.

For example, let's say that I am looking for a new executive assistant. I would prefer someone who can see the big picture, thinks innovatively, is not weighed down with a ton of detail and sees possibilities instead of limitations. This is a pretty good description of me – and a conversation with that person would most likely be enjoyable. However, if I was hiring an assistant to help me, I would actually need someone to handle the details, ground me in reality and take care of today's work, all while having some grasp of the big picture.

If I interviewed the first person I described, we would have a great conversation, I would feel very good about them and about myself, and I would be able to share my excitement for growth and innovation. It would serve my intellectual and social needs. But, the interview is not about filling my needs; it's about filling a position in my company.

Ask yourself:

- When I interview, am I clear about what qualities the position requires?

- Do I focus on finding that information as I interview?

- What would I like to hear from this person that may be unrelated to the job?

- What are qualities that I admire overall that may not be as important in this position?

- Am I aware of the fundamental values that someone must possess to work in my company

– yet know that it takes more than those values to do the tasks associated with the position for which I am hiring?

The interview itself is an opportunity to match that person with the job requirements, and not an opportunity to fill your personal needs – that's what your friends and family are for. Maybe you'd like to give them a call before your next interview.... ☺

Reading inspires thought.
Thought leads to ideas.
Ideas generate action.
Action happens one step at a time.
The first step is the most difficult
to determine and to take.

What are the first steps you will take as a result of reading this article?

1. _____
2. _____
3. _____

The Growth Image

"It's *disturbing* how much what you wear affects your customers and your employees!" This realization dawned on one of my clients years ago when he made a significant change in how he presented himself. Realizing that approachability could be maintained while commanding respect with what he wore, he saw what he called "disturbingly" significant results when he made a change from a polo shirt and khakis to a business suit.

We are not talking about avoiding major fashion mistakes; we are often talking about stepping it up to a suit or tie. Your results are affected by the presentation of yourself and your employees. Employees reflect you to a great degree. You may think of your company as having a relaxed and friendly atmosphere, and desire to be inviting to customers and comfortable for employees. And that's okay as long as you are watchful not to slip into contentment with comfortable and mediocre results.

I hear many "Yeah, buts..." about "my company" being different and how casual works. So, I challenge you to take a look at the results you are achieving:

- Are your customers chatty and spend more of your time than is profitable for you?

- Are your employees productive?

- Are your employees always respectful of you and your managers? In other words, do they consistently take direction from you and get things done as you request?

- Do you hear resistance from employees and customers when you make improvements in a system or increase efficiency in order to improve operations?

Identify the current balance between approachability and fun, and productivity and growth in your company. If the former outweighs the latter and you are not happy with the results, one seemingly small move you could make is to change how you and your team are dressed. Do you command respect? Do you exude confidence and focus? Do you attract like-minded thought?

Reading inspires thought.
Thought leads to ideas.
Ideas generate action.
Action happens one step at a time.
The first step is the most difficult
to determine and to take.

What are the first steps you will take as a result of reading this article?

1. _____

2. _____

3. _____

Stay on Target!

Have you ever modified job duties to fit a current employee's strengths or to avoid their weaknesses? *Oh, no!* When you do this, you risk deviating from your established goals and strategies.

Based on what you want to accomplish, and how you want to operate, you have divided responsibilities and established a work flow. Being an intelligent leader, you are open to the need to rearrange duties or adjust work flow based on new information and insights. However, these changes require strategic decisions and should not be based solely on what *might* achieve greater productivity or performance from a *particular* employee.

When you want to tweak a job for an employee, determine your motivation for doing so. Ask yourself:

- Am I avoiding coaching or disciplining this employee?

- Is this the right employee for *this* job?

- Would operations really flow better if I made this adjustment?

- What goal or strategy caused me to assign duties this way initially?

- What new information have I obtained or observations have I made to indicate it is time to change this job?

If you really want to move your team forward, you must set the direction, discover the best strategies to get there, assign tasks and responsibilities, and only tweak them when you have realized there truly is a better way to accomplish your goals.

Reading inspires thought.
Thought leads to ideas.
Ideas generate action.
Action happens one step at a time.
The first step is the most difficult
to determine and to take.

What are the first steps you will take as a result of reading this article?

1. _____
2. _____
3. _____

Maybe Poor Hiring Decisions Are Not To Blame

To be successful, you must hire the right people. They must be hired based on more than a gut feeling no matter how well you think you are able to read people to determine if they fit what is most important to the job.

Everyone hired by a company must also have an effective manager. Even two people who work together as partners still need to 'manage' their relationship. Management can be a dirty word because it may denote a hierarchy. Management is often defined using words like, 'handling,' 'dominating,' 'controlling,' and 'directing.'

Maybe the turnover, lack of performance or failure of your team to be *as great as they could be* may not be due to bad hiring decisions. Greatness in companies comes from the work of each and every member of the team *and* the leadership of the management team.

Steps to Take Upon Hire

When you hire someone new, you or your managers need to take these steps:

1. Make sure they receive a copy of the Job Description before they accept the job.

2. Make them feel welcome on Day One. Create a written training program including both minimum milestones and ambitious targets.

3. Make sure they have access to key people, even busy ones, so they can ask questions.

4. Set times for them to receive specific feedback daily, weekly or at a very minimum monthly for the first six months. That feedback is best in writing and should take place in a one-on-one conversation without distractions.

5. Continue to challenge the new employee. Focus on tasks on the horizon beyond what they are currently able to handle so they don't fall into a mode of being content and mediocre performers.

6. Ask for their feedback on processes and systems. Listen to their questions on processes in order to use their 'new eyes' to see things differently and improve.

7. Keep them on the radar of the supervisor or manager for at least the first six months based on a written training program. Even if they do very well, you can't afford to ignore them.

Even the best new hire needs leadership and management from their supervisor. How can you make sure it happens?

Reading inspires thought.
Thought leads to ideas.
Ideas generate action.
Action happens one step at a time.
The first step is the most difficult
to determine and to take.

What are the first steps you will take as a result of reading this article?

1. _____

2. _____

3. _____

Effective Leaders within your Company

It is important to empower employees. Equally critical is empowering leaders in an organization, whether it be managers, leaders, or front line supervisors and giving them responsibility not only for tasks, but for the people who report to them.

Delegating responsibility and trusting those managers is a very powerful way to bring out the best in them. However, two pieces need to be present for this to be successful.

1. Clear communication of your expectations.

2. Preparing the person to be able to handle the tasks and responsibilities.

Probably the skill most often not present, but continuously delegated, is the management and leadership of people. Few people come hard-wired to be able to lead a group well. Yet, there is nothing we assume more frequently than an individual's ability to lead others to accomplish results!

Whether you have one leader or supervisor in your small company or if you have a team of managers who report to you, do an inventory of the challenges they face and the areas in which you would like to see them and their team improve. Then look at their ability to lead the team and determine if that is the obstacle to achieving success. It may not be the processes, systems, technical abilities or employees' skills that are the problem.

Each of us is a unique person and people are a challenge to bring together seamlessly as a team. Recognize what leadership challenges your managers face and address them. You might decide to coach them yourself, send them to training or bring in assistance from the outside. Whatever you choose, be careful not to assume that the leadership part of their job is a non-issue when you are not getting the results you desire from their team.

Reading inspires thought.
Thought leads to ideas.
Ideas generate action.
Action happens one step at a time.
The first step is the most difficult
to determine and to take.

What are the first steps you will take as a result of reading this article?

1. _____
2. _____
3. _____

HOW not *IF*

Inspiring Employees
Section Overview

Based on how our brains are wired, it is so much easier to do something than to not do something. Therefore, the power of positive feedback to reinforce what you *want* your employees to do, or continue doing, is incredibly powerful. That requires your focus, attention, and time. It is often seen as optional and as a nicety, not as a critical component of management. People are inspired by those who take an interest in them, push them to excel and give them positive feedback. Create the dialog with employees to hear their input and recognize their contributions.

You may believe that your interactions with employees do not have the power to inspire and wonder 'If' these conversations are worth having. Even though they are positive conversations about what is going right, they can still be difficult conversations to have and to remember to make a part of your daily routine. The articles in this section highlight the importance of listening and communicating well, and 'How' that will enable you to inspire better and better performance.

With the determination to become a more inspiring leader, let's explore 'How,' not 'If' to get it done, one step at a time.

Reading the Signals

As you sit in your living room, for a moment think about the multitude of signals that are in the air around you that you can't see like radio waves, television signals, satellite transmissions and cell phone signals. Communication is happening all around you, most of which you never notice. When you turn on your cell phone, the signal that has been traveling through the room suddenly makes your cell phone ring. Now that you have the receptor (cell phone) on, you can receive the signal/ring that, until now, you were unaware existed.

Signals in the Workplace
In the workplace, as a leader or manager, you are surrounded by just as many signals. Employees are constantly sending verbal and nonverbal signals. Many leaders never turn on their receptors to receive the many signals that are in the air around them.

Employees are motivated by acknowledgement. When their accomplishments are recognized, their ideas and suggestions are respected, and their concerns are acknowledged and addressed, their motivation and commitment levels increase. Until the employee sees the leader's genuine interest in them, they may not be committed to what is important to the leader or the company. *A leader needs to care about how people feel and be exuberant in showing that!*

An effective leader wants to listen to employees, is available to hear their comments, recognizes their contributions, and is willing to act on their suggestions.

In order to genuinely be interested in what employees have to say, a leader must believe that the employees have valuable suggestions. Not all employees will offer record-breaking suggestions, but what they do suggest is particularly valuable because it is based on their daily work on the front lines.

Ask for Input

If you don't ask, your employees will assume you don't want to know, and won't tell you. There might be signals from alien planets that are in the air around us, but we have not discovered receptors for those messages yet. Managers may often feel like their employees are alien to them, and learning to receive those messages can be difficult. What to do? Ask!

In order to hear ideas and to ask for suggestions, the leader must be available and spend time with employees.

Publicly praise good ideas, recognizing the employee and team who made the suggestion. It will enhance your credibility and reward the employee, at no cost to anyone.

Take Action

Be ready and willing to act on what employees communicate with you. You may not be able to act on the information today or even this month, but be prepared to act and honestly tell the employee you will consider the suggestion. The goal of hearing these suggestions is not necessarily to implement them all. It is to learn what the employees are thinking, utilize the idea if it fits within the organization's strategy, and allow the employees a voice in their work environment.

It takes time and effort to listen to and implement suggestions. And this may be the most important time you spend all day. If concerns and complaints can be turned into opportunities for improvement that increase productivity and potentially save the company millions of dollars, you'd like to hear them! Then, ask questions, listen to the answers, recognize contributions, and be willing to act. The result will be a more dedicated team of employees, all striving for company success.

Reading inspires thought.
Thought leads to ideas.
Ideas generate action.
Action happens one step at a time.
The first step is the most difficult
to determine and to take.

What are the first steps you will take as a result of reading this article?

1. _____
2. _____
3. _____

How to Lead Happiness

You have the ability to influence your happiness by your actions. Happiness also has the potential to add ten years to your life, is contagious and there is no scientific correlation to age, gender or income.

How can you as a leader help others to find happiness? When I look around, I don't generally see a majority of people exude happiness. Can you affect that? And if you did, would that positively affect the team with which you work?

Confidence and Contentment

Although I don't claim to know the whole answer to those questions, I firmly believe that happiness comes from the confidence and contentment that a person possesses. In a happy person, this confidence leads to the belief that whatever might be frustrating or challenging at this moment, will be overcome through their positive approach to life and belief in their ability to affect their own situation.

If this is true, then as a leader, you have an opportunity to positively affect the happiness of your team. As the boss, you have a pretty significant ability to influence how the employee feels about themselves. You also have an awesome platform from which to encourage the employee to strive to achieve greatness.

If you wish to positively affect the employees' confidence, contentment and belief in their ability to achieve greatness:

- You can spend time listening to your employees in order to learn what makes them tick. Find out what is important to them. Engage them in conversation and listen. You may think you could ask, "What is really important to you?" or, "What motivates you?" and the employee will give you an accurate answer. But most people are not introspective to the point that they can relay this information in detail without having a discussion about what is *really* important to them. That is why money is often the first answer. Rarely would someone turn it down!

- You can set the expectation that they will focus on their own professional development. Encourage them to discuss with you, and get excited about, initiatives to improve their knowledge, skills and performance. As they make efforts and achieve milestones, you celebrate their efforts and reward their successes. Believe it or not, many people do not come into the workplace knowing how to achieve greatness. Your ability to lead them in this process will contribute to their happiness.

How do you currently contribute to others' happiness? What do you do to enable your employees to be happier than when they first came to work for you?

Reading inspires thought.
Thought leads to ideas.
Ideas generate action.
Action happens one step at a time.
The first step is the most difficult
to determine and to take.

What are the first steps you will take as a result of reading this article?

1. _____

2. _____

3. _____

Powerful Praise

The power of recognizing what people do *right* is immense! Yes, do something nice for employees during the holidays and on special days, and yes, write effective performance evaluations that praise their good behaviors as well as point out their need to improve. But, even more powerful and for greater impact, have the right day-to-day conversations with your employees. Every word that comes out of your mouth works to create the picture of how they see themselves, their job, their worth at the company and how motivated they are to take initiative and do what you expect.

Daily Conversations
There is enormous opportunity to shape the behavior and performance of your employees with your daily conversations. One of the most difficult things to do is to take what and how you want things done and translate it accurately from your brain to your employees' actions. And recognition of desired behaviors is *much, much* more powerful than correction of inappropriate behaviors or things not done how you want them done.

Whether it is a poor performer you resist firing or a great performer who you wish would do things just a little bit different, recognizing things they do well, big and small, *every day* is the key to changing their behavior.

1. Realize and admit how particular you are about the results you want, how you want to do business and how you want your company to operate.

2. Have brief conversations with people about, and thank them for, *little things* they are doing *right*.

3. Talk to them *daily* – reinforcing the culture you want to create.

If the picture in your mind of how your company or department should operate is bigger and better than it is operating right now and that bugs you, follow the three steps above – it may be more talking than you've done in a long time!

What Do I Say?

Be sincere in your praise and genuine in your curious questions.
I noticed you/great job on/congrats on [tasks/project/step]!
[on time/on budget] – how did you manage that?
I bet that is going to have a positive impact on [company goal or objective]? (ask as a question)
Of what part are you most proud?

This is impressive; I'd like to share those results with [boss, stakeholders]. Do you mind if I do, or would you like to tell them yourself?

That was a tough one, you've been working on that for a while – what did you do to finally make it work?

Was there anyone who worked hard alongside you on much of that?

Reading inspires thought.
Thought leads to ideas.
Ideas generate action.
Action happens one step at a time.
The first step is the most difficult
to determine and to take.

What are the first steps you will take as a result of reading this article?

1. _____

2. _____

3. _____

I Know You Can Do It!

"*I know you can do it!*" Why are these powerful words? When voiced by a manager, they express confidence in an employee. Despite the independent, sometimes egotistical approach of many employees, I believe there is a great lack of self-confidence under the surface, being hidden by confident speech. When someone who they respect, whether because of a great relationship or an official boss/subordinate relationship, believes the employee can do something, it energizes that employee.

You are telling them that you believe in them and that they should believe in themselves. Too mushy for you? Well, it's powerful and when used well, can bring about significant changes in performance.

"*I know you can do it!*" Do you tell your employees this? Do you tell your challenging employees this? Can you convince yourself to believe it for those who have less than stellar performance?

Why would you say this if you don't believe it 100%? There is power in what we say about ourselves and what others say about us. By saying, "I know you can do it," you are instilling a feeling of determination in the employee. And you will find the most success when you follow up by holding them accountable to taking steps to succeed.

When they Fail

What if they fail? Doesn't that mean you were wrong? No! It just depends on what timeframe you are talking about. If you say they can accomplish something and they are frustrated because they didn't finish in a week, push harder. Insist you know they can do it and ask them what they are going to do next to make progress. Everything is accomplished with a series of small steps.

Employees may at first try to prove you wrong in order to stay in their current comfortable level of performance. Insist you believe they can do what needs to be done, and that they have the ability to learn and to accomplish more than they have in the past.

Try it

Say, "I know you can do it!" with conviction to each employee once a week, follow up and hold them accountable, and see what happens!

Reading inspires thought.
Thought leads to ideas.
Ideas generate action.
Action happens one step at a time.
The first step is the most difficult
to determine and to take.

What are the first steps you will take as a result of reading this article?

1. _____
2. _____
3. _____

Inexpensive Ways to Say Thank You

You could write 'Thank you" on their Facebook wall, send a Text, 'Like' their work on LinkedIn, or drop them an email, but how about a few more old fashioned ways of saying "Thank you"?

1. Say it! Give them a call for no other reason than to say "Thank you!" If they are within walking distance, walk to their desk and say, "Thank you!" *And make sure you are specific about what it is you are thankful for.*

Everyone likes to be thanked, but it has a greater impact when you are specific. They cannot read your mind.

2. Write a handwritten thank you note. Again, be specific about what it is you appreciate. Include a $5 gift card to their favorite coffee shop.

3. Send that handwritten note to their home address, so they open it with family or friends nearby and receive further acknowledgment.

4. If they are paid hourly, give them an hour, half-day or day off with pay. It seems like the

most valuable commodity today is our time. There are so many demands upon it. Give something very valuable to them!

5. Recognition in a staff meeting of their peers. Not everyone likes public praise, but in a staff meeting of peers, where the comment is specific and linked to business results, the impact can be very powerful.

6. Start a thank you card for every employee. Ask every employee to put a note of specific thanks in each card other than their own. Add your note to the card as well. You may ask them to start their note with, "I rely on you for..." or "Thank you for…" or "I appreciate you for…." When I have done this, it has done wonders for teambuilding as well as improved employee morale.

7. Encourage an employee to say or write a thank you note to a fellow employee. Ensure they include the specifics of what they are thankful for.

8. Buy a small "perfect" gift for someone. When you buy something small but well suited to their likes or hobbies, it means you have been listening to what is important to them. It doesn't need to cost much. Are they a big sports fan? Do they love movies, but never pick up a book? Have you been listening enough to do this? Leave the gift on their desk with a little note.

9. Pass along a compliment from a client. Put it in writing, share it with their boss or peers, and

tell them what keeping that client happy means to the business overall.

10. Wash their car - without them knowing while they are at work. Getting your hands dirty is a great way to show your dedication and appreciation.

11. Cook them hamburgers and hot dogs on the grill at lunch time. Especially if they work a different shift than you, they will appreciate the food and especially enjoy seeing you at their 2:00am lunch time.

Reading inspires thought.
Thought leads to ideas.
Ideas generate action.
Action happens one step at a time.
The first step is the most difficult
to determine and to take.

What are the first steps you will take as a result of reading this article?

1. _____
2. _____
3. _____

Christmas Bonuses – Are They a Good Idea?

Christmas Bonuses are frequently discussed, and often given at companies both large and small to their employees at the end of the calendar year. It is the season of giving and no employee in their right mind would turn them down. But, are they a good idea? They are if you adhere to the following guidelines.

Bonuses:

Be very clear what the bonus is for. If it is based on performance, then make sure it is determined by individual, measurable (and actually measured) performance indicators. If it is based on company performance, make sure to communicate what, in particular, each employee did to contribute to the success of the company over the last period.

This is as simple as putting specifics in a note enclosed with the bonus check, and/or having a discussion with them about the basis of the bonus when you hand them the check. This way, the employee will know specifically what to do or to continue to do to impact their bonus (and your bottom line) next year.

Gifts:

If you don't tell the employee what the bonus is for, it will be considered a gift, and they will automatically expect it to happen and probably increase every year.

If you give pure gifts (not based on individual or company performance) to employees, keep them relatively consistent in value from year to year. If given a smaller gift one year than the last, they will automatically wonder what they did differently to deserve a different gift, wonder if the company is not doing well or if you are upset with them or their performance.

Remember, employees are reading the signals you are sending and money does send its messages. Your best bet? If you're going to give a gift, be consistent and call it a gift. If you're going to give a bonus, tie it to something valuable to your company's desired results.

Reading inspires thought.
Thought leads to ideas.
Ideas generate action.
Action happens one step at a time.
The first step is the most difficult
to determine and to take.

What are the first steps you will take as a result of reading this article?

1. _____
2. _____
3. _____

Credibility

Do you do what you say you will do?

We would all like to think the answer to that question is a resounding, "Yes!" As a leader, doing what you say you will do plays a significant role in building your credibility with your constituents.

It's very easy to follow through on concrete promises such as, "Next month, I will buy you the new software you need." You can easily evaluate whether or not you did what you said you would do. However, in order to build credibility and trust with your employees, you must look at all the messages they receive from you. Do you have a mission statement, customer service standards or long-term goals for your company? Have you remained focused on these 'promises' and have you done what you said your company would do? Have you communicated changes in the plan? Are there any permissible exceptions to your standards?

In order to do what you say you will do, make sure you keep track of any and all promises you make to employees, especially those like, "I'll look into that and get back to you," since you make those promises when you are very busy. Increase your awareness of all the messages that you are sending to employees every day. As a manager, you see many opportunities you would like to seize, get excited about them, and picture yourself succeeding in those areas. Employees, on the other hand, do not have as much independence and need to rely on you to feel secure and believe in what you say you will do.

It is lonely at the top! Most often, employees do not share the leader's desire to constantly look for the next opportunity and may see your proclamation that we are going to do things 'this' way now, or we are going to operate according to 'these' standards, as promises that they can use as the basis for how to perform well. They expect you to stick to what you have said and reward their good performance.

Are you credible? What messages are you sending? What messages do you want your employees to receive?

Reading inspires thought.
Thought leads to ideas.
Ideas generate action.
Action happens one step at a time.
The first step is the most difficult
to determine and to take.

What are the first steps you will take as a result of reading this article?

1. _____

2. _____

3. _____

HOW <u>not</u> *IF*

Professional Improvement

Section Overview

The best leaders and managers are those who focus on their own professional development. This professional development is not only about attending seminars. It involves identifying areas of strength and potential and setting individual goals for growth. Identifying what to improve may be the most difficult step and is often skipped. Opportunities are seized as they arise instead of identifying needs first and seeking options that are the best fit. *You* know *you* best and although others' input is valid, you have the greatest insight into your true strengths and opportunities. Beating stress, developing employees, improving decision making or managing your time better are all areas that are critical to your success and opportunities for performance improvement. If you are willing to accept decent or mediocre performance from yourself (deciding 'If' you will improve), you will be sacrificing potential greatness of which you are capable. Instead, spend time determining 'How' you will improve, accepting the challenge to uncover a level of skill, talent and strength you did not realize you possessed.

This section includes a series of articles that offer insights into key areas of development. These areas can all have a powerful impact on your interactions with others. The more you are prepared mentally, emotionally and intellectually to interact with others, the better you will be able to navigate the most difficult conversations.

With the determination to focus on professional improvement, let's explore 'How,' not 'If' to get it done, one step at a time.

Beating Stress on a Daily Basis

When people experience chronic stress, their ability to think clearly is diminished. They have the tendency to make bad long term decisions.

The best leaders take their responsibilities most seriously and therefore are susceptible to higher levels of stress. And as important as it is to take that nice summer vacation, it is certainly not going to fix everything. The same pressures and problems remain when you return and often they exist 24 hours a day, seven days a week, depending on the intensity of your leadership role.

No matter how talented you are, how effective you might be, and what high energy and dedication you exude, your body is still human and experiences limits at which your productivity and performance suffer when you reach certain amounts of prolonged stress.

Lower Your Stress Level
Do something proactive every day to lower your level of stress.

1. Identify *when* it is for you that your productivity decreases. When do you lose your edge, or begin to be less sharp in your decision making and performance?

2. Know *what* stresses you. Everyone is different in what causes them to be stressed. This is based on your personality, your experiences and history, and your way of thinking. I have seen great variety in what triggers a particular leader's stress levels. It may be mainly situations of personal conflict, ensuring happy customers, holding others accountable, financial complexity, attention to detail, or inability to see the big picture – sometimes with far less concern about other variables.

3. What allows you to *refocus?* It doesn't need to be something that is 'in style' or 'hip'. And it may not be relaxation, exercise or sleep. Yes, you need these things to live a healthy life, but they may not be the things that specifically help you refocus when you have lost your edge due to stress. What can you do in 15 minutes every day to release your stress? Maybe it is reading a fictional book, meditating, planning, writing, playing a mindless game of solitaire, going for a leisurely stroll, power walking, being alone, praying, or calling a friend. For me personally, it's getting something done, no matter how small. There is a difference between what is good for you and what you enjoy; and the particular things that can refocus you when stress has caused you to lose your edge.

Taking care of yourself through diet, exercise and relaxation are critical. Doing what you enjoy and having fun is very important. Knowing what you can do in the moment of overload to refocus and get back on task effectively is often overlooked and is just as critical! If you don't know, ask others what they do, try something suggested here and spend the 15 minutes a day finding what it is for you, so when you need that relief, you know what to do.

Reading inspires thought.
Thought leads to ideas.
Ideas generate action.
Action happens one step at a time.
The first step is the most difficult
to determine and to take.

What are the first steps you will take as a result of reading this article?

1. _____
2. _____
3. _____

Where Does Your 'Can Do' Attitude End?

If you're like most ambitious leaders and managers, you have a pretty strong 'can do' attitude.

When you set a goal or see an opportunity of interest to you, you set the direction, get the wheels turning, involve others and go! Your vocabulary probably does not include "can't" "impossible" or "that won't work."

Yet I find that even the most ambitious leaders may use those phrases when they speak about certain members of their team. And it may be true about those individuals who may not be the best fit for your team. But think about it. Does your 'can do' attitude end when it comes to the professional development of your team members? I don't mean sending them to training seminars, offering flex time as they work toward a degree or holding workshops in-house. These are all very important components of professional development, but what about your ability as the leader to help them individually develop?

Individual Employee Development

This requires:

- Your ambitious vision of what they could achieve, your insight into their undeveloped skills, and your confidence and belief in the potential they possess which has not yet been uncovered.

- Your conversation with them about what they believe they are capable of achieving.

- Your work with them to set specific goals with measurable results and clear deadlines for them to achieve.

- Your follow up to hold them accountable to what you both believe they are capable of improving, and the specific actions they have agreed to complete.

Does your "can do" attitude extend to your belief about your ability to develop others? Do you have any interest in personally interacting with them in order to do so? Although as a leader of your team, you take the leadership of your *team* seriously, the *team* is not a living, breathing person. And it doesn't have the same individuality, depth or personality that an *employee* possesses which adds complexity. So, it might be easier to come up with the next unique marketing strategy, work on a process or system to increase efficiency, or investigate ways to decrease expenses, than it is to successfully interact one-on-one with your key players to enable them to access their potential.

What have you done this quarter to personally work with key individuals in your organization to enhance their professional development?

Reading inspires thought.
Thought leads to ideas.
Ideas generate action.
Action happens one step at a time.
The first step is the most difficult
to determine and to take.

What are the first steps you will take as a result of reading this article?

1. _____
2. _____
3. _____

Personal Accountability

Do you take personal accountability for what happens with your team? Or do you find yourself blaming your employees?

Does this scenario sound familiar?
You set your department goals. They are ambitious, but doable. You have most of the right people in place and need to hire just one more person. You hire that person; tell the new hire and your current team about your great plans and everyone gets to work. First quarter passes and you can point out some successes, but you are behind on the goals.

You think to yourself, "Well, we have had some unusual challenges in the industry, my employees have not been fully on board, and budgets have been a little too tight to do some of the things we wanted to."

You keep everyone posted on the progress year-to-date and know they will get moving this second quarter. They'd better, or you will have a serious talk with them.

It's almost the end of the second quarter and you're still not reaching the targets. This happened last year too and you're determined to not let it happen again! You talk to your employees and they are full of excuses, ensuring you they are working hard, they just need some more training, and you know they are so busy right now....

A young man had a desire to change the world!

When he was in his 20's he prayed, "God, there is so much need all around me, I pray that I can change the world!" In his 40's, the man had not changed the world, so he prayed again, "God, please let me change everyone I come in contact with." By his 60's he was disappointed, but a bit wiser, and realized he hadn't been able to change everyone else. Then he prayed, "God, please help me to just change *me* before I die."

When you realize that major change comes from looking inside first, then you are able to maximize your impact on the world and on your team. What do you want to improve about yourself as a leader?

Could some of the lack of success described in the scenario above be because of you and your desire to change everyone else? What do ***you*** need to work to improve?

- Do your goals for the year include what you want to do better as a manager? What you want to learn? How you want to grow as a leader? What are you doing to become a better manager and leader? Are you personally getting in the way of your team's success?

- Maybe in the scenario above, you didn't hire the right person, didn't orient them well, didn't train them appropriately, and didn't coach them effectively. Essentially, you expected to hire the perfect person who by osmosis learned everything about their role in the first two weeks.

- Maybe you are not good at setting realistic goals, communicating your goals, helping people understand and buy in, or leading people through implementation.

- Maybe you stink at the details of implementation and wish to be the idea-generator instead, but do not know how to best support the people you put in charge to implement. Maybe you put no one in charge to implement because you think the details are the easy part and you have people who should be able to handle those.

- Maybe you are not good at problem solving or decision making, and the perfect plan on paper written at the beginning of the year isn't so perfect anymore; yet you can't seem to turn it around.

- Maybe you are too demanding, unsure, impulsive, emotional, suspicious, aloof, complacent or arbitrary. Any number of endearing personality traits are an inherent part of us all. Some you have discovered and work around. Are some still a mystery to you?

Whatever your personal challenges might be, you'd better have a plan in place to address and improve on the things you don't do well. As much as it is important to lead the team according to your vision – which is incredibly powerful and valuable – it is just as important to take responsibility to improve what it is about you professionally that needs some work. It's hard to look at yourself. Have you done that recently?

Reading inspires thought.
Thought leads to ideas.
Ideas generate action.
Action happens one step at a time.
The first step is the most difficult
to determine and to take.

What are the first steps you will take as a result of reading this article?

1. _____
2. _____
3. _____

The Missing Step to Success

Do you expect exceptional performance from your employees? When you first hire them, they do not yet know the job, but do you have the expectation that once they are taught, they should perform close to perfect if you hired the right person?

As a leader, you retain responsibility for shaping those whom you hire. You need to be prepared to teach them. Depending on the depth and uniqueness of your expectations of their performance, you may need to do a good deal of teaching – which surprises many leaders. This is often what is missing when a company does not reach its potential for success.

Keep in mind that teaching does not always result in learning. Teaching is about you – deciding what they need to learn, planning how to teach them and delivering the information. Learning is about them – how do they learn and did they understand it? Are you, your key managers and your lead employees good at teaching in a way that results in learning?

What are the qualities and skills of a good trainer?

- Expert in the subject matter
- Understands learning styles of individuals
- Understands group dynamics & rapport
- Handles tough questions well
- Warm, understanding and enthusiastic
- Prepared, organized, and businesslike
- Imaginative and creative
- Uses relevant examples
- Listens, elicits conversation and demonstration of learning
- Measures learning comprehension
- Gives constructive feedback
- Desires to discover and rectify, "Whey don't they understand?"

Who trains your employees? Do your employees learn? How do you measure comprehension? How effective are you at training? Do you only think you are supporting employees and addressing their areas of poor performance or are you teaching for greater success? How do you measure success?

If you want to be successful as a leader, you must be prepared to teach those on your team.

Reading inspires thought.
Thought leads to ideas.
Ideas generate action.
Action happens one step at a time.
The first step is the most difficult
to determine and to take.

What are the first steps you will take as a result of reading this article?

1. _____
2. _____
3. _____

What are your Time Management Challenges?

Score yourself on a scale of 1 - 5 for each of the statements below, where 1 is "Not a problem," and 5 is "Oh yeah, that's me!!" Then, add up the numbers and find your score on the rating scale at the end of the quiz.

1 2 3 4 5   You are the bottleneck.

1 2 3 4 5   You are a perfectionist which makes it hard to finish things, and hard to let go or delegate.

1 2 3 4 5   You don't use a schedule or find it hard to stick to the one you created.

1 2 3 4 5   You are disorganized and get lost in what to do next.

1 2 3 4 5   You can't say "No" and end up doing unimportant things.

1 2 3 4 5   You are easily sidetracked, because you are uninterested in certain things or like to create but don't like the details.

1 2 3 4 5   You like 'shiny things' and new, exciting opportunities and possibilities take you off task.

1 2 3 4 5   Your goals are not clear and specific enough to guide your daily actions.

1 2 3 4 5   There are too many little things to do that fill up your day and the important things don't get done for lack of time.

1 2 3 4 5   There is always a crisis or deadline for you to handle or address.

1 2 3 4 5   You don't have a plan for how you want your week to ideally work.

1 2 3 4 5   You aren't very effective in communicating to others which causes a delay in getting things done or necessitates that you do it yourself.

1 2 3 4 5   When you think you have communicated something, you end up needing to clarify or have the conversation again at a later date.

1 2 3 4 5   You are not very good at project management - staying on top of all the things for which you are responsible.

1 2 3 4 5   The place you do your work is not always conducive to getting things done.

1 2 3 4 5   You get caught up in your work and before you know it, hours have passed since you looked at the clock or the day is over.

16 You are a time management genius. You have no problems getting things done!

17-30 You are doing really well. Give yourself a pat on the back for what you do well. Identify those key points where you could be even more effective, and make a little progress on those areas every week.

31-55 You get things done, but have a lot more potential. Meet with a boss, mentor, coach or peer and ask for some feedback. Pull out a personality assessment you may have done in the past. Get in touch with your preferences and see what light that sheds on your time management challenges. Make a concerted effort to set two or three goals and determine one or two action items for each to specifically improve your time management skills. Decide how you will reward yourself when you reach them. Identify your reason and motivation for wanting to improve, which may include more time with family, improved productivity, higher pay, increased happiness, or less stress.

56-79 Your time is probably not your own. Identify the top five statements that are most problematic for you. Create action items for each and hold yourself accountable to reaching them.

80 You are in big trouble! Take this entire list and make action items for each statement on how to improve.

Reading inspires thought.
Thought leads to ideas.
Ideas generate action.
Action happens one step at a time.
The first step is the most difficult
to determine and to take.

What are the first steps you will take as a result of reading this article?

1. _____

2. _____

3. _____

Time Management is Easy

Time Management is easy... all you must do is make the right decision every moment of every day.

In reaction to this definition of time management, I hear anything from "Impossible!" to "Maybe in an ideal world!" The fact is that as a leader, your time may be the most valuable asset you have, the component over which you have the most control, and the key strategic card you can play to positively affect your team.

Are you overcome with work? Do your customers determine your schedule? Do your employees' immediate needs usurp your overall goals?

Long term goals, current customer concerns and employees' needs are all critical to your team's success. However, as the leader you have the best ability to grasp the full array of priorities for the operations. You have the best ability to make decisions on which priorities are top priorities and will achieve the results you and your team are responsible to deliver.

Moments of Opportunity

Every moment of every day you have the opportunity to choose the best thing to do. However, the craziness of the day and the demands of others may lead you to keep busy and do many things, but not necessarily make the right decision of what needs to be done first and what can wait.

Planning your Day

Planning your day, especially on paper, is the first step to managing your time well. The next step is to address the many exceptions, changes and interruptions that will inevitably fill your day. When these things happen, stop in that moment and be an unemotional observer of the situation. If you were watching you, what would you tell yourself to do in order to make a good decision? You might say, "I know you want to do priority A, but priority B really should come first," or, "I know you are upset with Bob, but his request *is* higher priority," or, "Getting his work done is the right thing to do. He has been waiting for a while now."

Become an Observer

Step out of your rat race, be a fly on the wall and make the best objective decision of how to spend each moment of your day, focusing on the things you know are the biggest priorities. If your priorities are not clear, list all the types of tasks you do routinely, number them in order of priority and test the order by making all decisions according to that priority list for a few days. Then, adjust as necessary and use this as a guide in tough moments.

Seize every moment of your managerial life to make the best decisions for a focused and successful future.

Reading inspires thought.
Thought leads to ideas.
Ideas generate action.
Action happens one step at a time.
The first step is the most difficult
to determine and to take.

What are the first steps you will take as a result of reading this article?

1. _____

2. _____

3. _____

Top Ten Productivity Tips

Make the right decision every moment of every day
This definition of good time management is a realization that you make many decisions every day on how to spend your time, whether planned or unplanned. The more you can make those decisions consciously, and according to clear goals, the more productive you will be. Most people welcome distractions to some extent as a relief from something stressful, difficult or unpleasant. Act very purposefully in each moment of the day and pinpoint those times you tend to make decisions to do things, however small, that are not in line with your goals and correct that situation.

Revisit your goals
Dust them off. Clean them up. Do the reality check and adjust the ones that are unrealistic. Get excited again about ones that might be a stretch but about which you are passionate. Tweak others given your knowledge of the year to date. And if you never put them in writing, do it now.

Identify what must be done this month, this week, today and tomorrow to achieve your goals
One of the best ways to be productive and make the best use of your time is to be focused and plan. I'm not talking about the strategic five year plan. I'm talking about knowing the three or four non-routine things that you want to accomplish this month to ensure you are further ahead and closer to your goals than when you started the month. Then, decide what two or three things you need to do this week to make that happen. Look at your plan for today and tomorrow and decide what one or two things you need to do in those 24-48 hours to move forward on the week's goals.

Know your Best Time of Day
There is a time of day when you are most productive. Are you a morning person? Are you a night owl? Do you really wake up at noon? Observe your productivity and effectiveness. What time of day are you at your best? When you determine when that is, schedule your most important activities at that time. Avoid doing trivial tasks or putting out fires during that prime time.

Schedule your day, week and month
Very few of us have schedules that are never interrupted or rearranged. But, that is not a reason to skip planning. Plot out your month, schedule your week and map out your day. Leave some "Wing it" time to fit in the little things that will inevitably pop up. Schedule this block of time to do the emails and phone calls that fill your day if you are not careful. When at the end of the day you have not done everything you wanted to because of fires and interruptions,

immediately reschedule the activities that you did not do for tomorrow or later in the week. Be realistic and schedule time for the interruptions you know will occur and you will accept because of their importance.

Get rid of the Things to Do List
It haunts most of us. Instead of putting something on the list, schedule it somewhere in your day or week. Replace a less important task if you need to. If you cannot find anywhere to put it, that means it is really not important enough to you to do it, so don't torture yourself with leaving it to haunt you on a list. You may want to keep a "To Do Someday" List for those things that are great ideas, but are just not a priority right now. Then, put it away and only look at it periodically.

Schedule appointments to talk
If you plan to meet with another person and have a conversation, do it purposefully. If you just 'stop by' their office or give them a call without a plan, you may end up wasting both people's time. And they may do the same with you. If you need to talk to them, plan a time and day and have an agenda.

Do a time log
After you have planned your month, week and day, and taken all the Things To Do list items and scheduled them somewhere, for just a few days - record what you *actually* did. Compare your reality to your plan. Maybe you need to adjust how you do what you do, become more effective, learn to say, "No," or delegate more. Unless you have a good picture of what you are actually doing, it's hard to have a basis for pro-

ductive change. And no, you really don't know what you spend your time doing until you log it. Try it and you'll see!

Stop Procrastinating

Many managers and leaders are procrastinators. I never believed that about myself until I understood the connection between procrastinating and being a perfectionist. For the perfectionist, it is rarely ever the right time or there is not enough time to do it right, so some tasks are put off indefinitely. That is not to say that perfectionists are not productive, only that certain things that are new, different or particularly important are put off for the more immediate, urgent and familiar tasks at which they can more easily succeed.

Keep track of information.

You may mistake being able to do a lot with being organized. It's amazing how much time you spend looking for something, finding information twice, having a conversation or part of it a second time, or sorting through the volumes of information you use to do your job. Review your systems for collecting, sorting and using information. Do they effectively support your mission or do they slow you down?

Reading inspires thought.
Thought leads to ideas.
Ideas generate action.
Action happens one step at a time.
The first step is the most difficult
to determine and to take.

What are the first steps you will take as a result of reading this article?

1. _____
2. _____
3. _____

Tasks Most Critical

Which activities, tasks, or types of tasks that you perform on a routine basis are really and truly critical to your success?

Think of two equally important tasks that might arise at the same moment. You would decide which one to do first. How would you choose? If you had only one half hour to work today, what would you do with that time? What absolutely has to be done?

Fire-Fighting
If you answered the question above with very urgent or fire-extinguishing activities, your team is probably in fire-fighting mode. That makes it hard to look at longer term or bigger picture priorities because you must put out fires or the whole thing goes up in smoke.

Focus on Customers
If you have moved beyond fire-fighting, you may answer the above questions by prioritizing activities relating to taking care of current customers as most critical. Which specific activities or tasks that you do to take care of current internal and external customers are most critical? You could, in an extreme sense, spend 100%

of your time taking care of your current customers and addressing their every need. That would only work as a strategy if your current revenue and profit matches your definition of success *and* none of your customers will ever change the amount of business they do with you.

In the world of reality, you know you must balance taking care of current customers with doing all the other tasks necessary to success. For each organization, there is a formula for success where the relationship is profitable and business continues. You probably spend some time on marketing and selling your product or service. If you spent 100% of your time here however, your customers would become unhappy, you'd lose their business and would not receive referrals.

Critical, Important & Trivial

Look at the tasks you do each day, each week and each month. Categorize them as:

1. Critical – highly urgent and important

2. Important – determines long term success, or

3. Trivial – needs to be done at some time by someone, but that may not need to be you.

In order to put tasks into those categories you need to know what makes your organization tick. You may want to look at variables such as:

- Profit margin on each product or service, and identify the most profitable

- Where those customers came from

- What you did to make them come to you from those sources

- What affects the financial health of your department or company?

- Areas of risk - in your business and your industry

- What activities have you done that have resulted in the best performance from your employees?

- What's important to your customers? Why do they stay with you? They often cannot tell you this in a survey, because they can't put their finger on it themselves. You might need to take your best customers to lunch and ask insightful questions in order to learn what is truly important to them.

Once you have categorized your tasks into Critical, Important and Trivial, then ask:

- Can you increase the productivity or efficiency of less critical tasks?

- Can you increase your return on investment of time spent doing critical tasks?

- Can you delegate or stop doing trivial tasks?

- Can you prioritize important tasks that may free up time in the future?

- Can you proactively prevent critical fire fights, in order to free up your time to do important tasks that contribute to your long term success?

Reading inspires thought.
Thought leads to ideas.
Ideas generate action.
Action happens one step at a time.
The first step is the most difficult
to determine and to take.

What are the first steps you will take as a result of reading this article?

1. _____
2. _____
3. _____

HOW not IF

Effective Meetings
Section Overview

When you work with people, you need to talk to them. And when you need to talk to them, it probably makes sense to do so in a meeting at times. But so often, meetings and conversations are unproductive, and some of the most difficult conversations occur in meetings. That leads many professionals to avoid meetings entirely and meet as infrequently as possible and only as a last resort. At times, people do hold too many meetings. Sometimes the situation requires an 'If' question: "Should we hold this meeting?" Other times the situation would be best solved with a meeting of the right people, and the question is instead, "'How' do we make it most effective?"

This section includes articles on 'How' to lead a productive meeting that produces results and what types of meetings to hold. This information will help you to streamline the meetings you hold, prepare well, and lead meetings effectively.

With the determination to be able to lead more effective meetings, let's explore 'How,' not 'If' to get it done, one step at a time.

AGHHHH! Meetings!

"A meeting is an event at which the minutes are kept and the hours are lost."

- Gourd's Axiom

Have you ever been to an unproductive meeting? Have you ever been to a meeting that went too long? Does the word 'meeting' make your skin crawl?

Create an agenda.
Communicate clearly what you hope to accomplish and what will happen at the meeting. Make sure *you* know this before you call the meeting. If you don't have clarity, you probably don't need to meet at this point. Many meetings are called to address huge problems, but you must climb that mountain one step at a time. If your agenda will take six hours, decide on the first step or milestone and cover that in the first meeting.

Consider who to invite.
People with a reason and a role make the best participants. There may be reasons why you need to include certain people due to office politics, but the less the better.

Circulate the agenda.
Indicate who is expected to participate and indicate at what point in the agenda you require their participation. Expect preparation on the part of the attendees. Instead of creating an agenda item like 'Sales Performance,' consider having each person prepare to present their relevant numbers, new initiatives, progress and one challenge. Ask them come prepared to report and indicate their participation requirements on the agenda. If you don't have the authority to require their participation, have someone with the authority 'reply all' voicing their agreement with the expectation that everyone come prepared.

Start on time. End on time. Prohibit interruptions.
Tell everyone you will start and end on time and stay true to your word. Communicate that everyone will be expected to stay during the meeting - leaving even for a three minute phone call may require you repeat information upon their return. People will appreciate this stringency because their time will be well spent.

Stay on agenda.
Set time limits for each item and assign someone the role of timekeeper.

Accomplish the results you said you would.
If your plan was to discover new strategies to address slumping sales, then ensure before everyone leaves that strategies have been generated, responsibilities and deadlines have been assigned, accountability measures have been put into action, and follow-up timeframes have been clearly identified. Have someone record and distribute this information.

Address the elephants in the room.

If someone is taking the meeting off track, or is obviously negative or thwarting progress with their participation, address it. Everyone will appreciate it. "Mark, I'm hearing that you have some serious concerns about our ability to increase sales. We are addressing today *how* we will do that, not *if* we will. It's important we get all our ideas on the table before we decide that they will not work. Their viability could be covered in a future meeting. I'd be happy to speak with you after this meeting to address your concerns before that future conversation. Does that work for you?"

Meetings do not run themselves and assembling a group of great people in a room never guarantees that *anything* will get accomplished, especially what you *want* to accomplish. Only call a meeting if you need one and can adhere to the above guidelines.

Reading inspires thought.
Thought leads to ideas.
Ideas generate action.
Action happens one step at a time.
The first step is the most difficult
to determine and to take.

What are the first steps you will take as a result of reading this article?

1. _____
2. _____
3. _____

Yes! Meetings!

As maddening as meetings can be, there are three types that I believe do need to happen without fail, and must be done well to keep things running smoothly.

The **Executive Team** meeting:

- *This includes* executive team members which may include the owner and their top four or five key people, the co-owners of a business, or maybe just a single owner themselves. Yes, I am suggesting you meet with yourself. This could also be the director and managers at a middle level of an organization who are the executive team of that facility, division or department.

- *The purpose* is to set goals, review successes and progress toward existing goals, and identify short term priorities. Even though you may routinely communicate effectively with whoever is on your executive team, you still need to set aside time where goals are evaluated, set or reset, and priorities are established to ensure you reach those goals before too much time slips by.

- *If this meeting is not held*, limited success may be achieved, but excuses are allowed, minimal progress is accepted, distraction often occurs, and at the end of the year, an unpleasant surprise of unmet goals may await the leaders.

The **Undivided Attention** meetings:
- *This includes* meetings between each employee and their direct supervisor and should occur on a routine monthly basis. If you have too many direct reports to make this happen, then change the reporting structure. The employees need you and your attention!

- *The purpose* is to continue to challenge your employees to improve their performance with your support. They report their successes, their challenges, and what they are working on and working to improve upon. Then you give them feedback on the same and determine ongoing priorities and action items together.

- *If this meeting is not held*, you may never improve your less than stellar performers and you may lose your top performers if they don't feel challenged. Everyone needs time from their supervisor that is focused on them and their performance. A yearly evaluation is not enough.

The **Problem Solving** meeting:
- *This includes* the stakeholders in the problem you are trying to solve. Be sure to include all involved stakeholders, and try not to include anyone who does not need to be there.

- *The purpose* is to solve a particular, well defined problem. Maybe the first step in solving that problem is to define it well. That may be the sole purpose of the meeting. If your problem is employee turnover, the first problem solving meeting may be to define what information needs to be gathered and who should gather it in order to analyze the breadth and depth of the turnover problem.

- *If this meeting is not held*, bandaids may be applied to a problem, ambitious individuals will take steps to solve a problem and the efforts will be uncoordinated. For some problems this initiative taken by individuals may work fine and be a great way to solve the problem. Other times it will be a disconnected way to look at an overall problem that would be best solved most quickly by bringing the right people together and putting the plan in place.

If you fail to hold these three types of meetings, you are certainly not alone, but you may be missing some of the focus, concerted effort, and exponential results that come from well planned and well placed meetings.

Reading inspires thought.
Thought leads to ideas.
Ideas generate action.
Action happens one step at a time.
The first step is the most difficult
to determine and to take.

What are the first steps you will take as a result of reading this article?

1. _____
2. _____
3. _____

Best Meetings - Small Scope, Big Expectations!

Have you ever been to or led a meeting that ran really long in an effort to make it through the whole agenda? Or one that ended on time but most agenda items, including the ones you were interested in, were never addressed?

Every time you have several people in a room, you have multiple priorities, opinions, preferences and styles which will ensure that nothing will be done as quickly as you are able to do alone. However, the richness of those dynamics is worth the tradeoff, but your expectations must be realistic.

First, you must expect people to want to share their opinions and concerns, and time must be built into the agenda for that to happen. If they are expected to simply sit and listen, then that must be communicated ahead of time to avoid frustrations. If you'd like to guide their participation, add specific bullet points to the agenda in order to do so.

Define the Scope

Then, you must define the scope of the meeting to be small enough to realistically be completed. People like to walk out of a meeting feeling successful. If your expectation of what you can complete in 45 minutes is always too high, and nothing ever seems to be resolved, your participants will get frustrated, you will lose credibility and productivity will decrease further.

Consider what you expect to accomplish; then break it into parts. You wish to discuss Project A. Project A has many parts. Maybe the scope of the first meeting is to identify the main parts of the project, the key activities, define the milestones and pinpoint the responsible people. The responsible people could get together at a future meeting to discuss their individual accountabilities and timeframes. Keep the scope manageable within your meeting timeframe.

Big Expectations

Small scope does not mean small expectations. When you discuss Project A, your expectation may be that it is approached from several new directions, everyone contributes to identifying key activities, and each person excitedly accepts a key role and milestones are clearly defined, which are all challenges in many companies.

In order to realize those ambitious expectations, they must be communicated prior to the meeting in a written agenda, and possibly an invitation phone call; must be reiterated in the agenda and at the start of the meeting, and revisited throughout the meeting as they are accomplished.

A small scope in no way means that very little will be accomplished. It simply means that you will do an amazing job of discussing, brainstorming and working on results relating to a small piece of a larger puzzle.

If your meetings appear unproductive, remember Small Scope, Big Expectations!

Reading inspires thought.
Thought leads to ideas.
Ideas generate action.
Action happens one step at a time.
The first step is the most difficult
to determine and to take.

What are the first steps you will take as a result of reading this article?

1. _____
2. _____
3. _____

About the Author

Bridget DiCello is an expert in getting things done by effectively navigating difficult conversations. She inspires leaders to take action in the relationships most important to their business and their success. Bridget's presentations are described as innovative, motivational, and focused on solving real world business problems with solutions that can be implemented immediately. Bridget's passion for effective leadership, exponential company growth and enabling both managers and employees to reach their potential is evident in the focused yet energizing coaching, training and seminars for which she is known.

Bridget is also the author of OPPORTUNITY SPACE™. For nearly a decade, Bridget has been working with executive teams and professionals using her powerful concept of Opportunity Space to transform their teams and their businesses.

Bridget brings 15 plus years of experience-from running Nursing Homes and Retirement Communities to coaching executive teams in small businesses, mid-size companies, Fortune 100 and Inc. 500 firms. Born and raised in snowy Buffalo, New York, Bridget currently resides in Memphis, Tennessee. Her education includes a Master's in Business Administration from the University at Buffalo, a Bachelor of Science in Business Administration and Health Planning and Management from Alfred University, and she is a Certified Training Professional, a designation received from the University of Mississippi.

Bridget@BridgetDiCello.com | www.bridgetdicello.com

Index